"After many years of treating children with cancer and comforting their parents, Dr. Komp is most able to answer the deep questions with divine as well as human sensitivity and truth."

LUIS PALAU, author, *Where Is God When Bad Things Happen?*

"Too bad Job did not have Diane Komp as his attending physician! This fine book makes it clear that she is a wonderful companion to all who struggle with the mysteries of suffering."

RICHARD J. MOUW, author, *Uncommon Decency*

"The book of Job teaches us how to believe when the unbelievable happens; how to reach up when you're trampled down; how to know God when you doubt there is a God to know; and how to use the encouragement of others to be a minister of mercy in a cruel world. Dr. Komp helps us translate a true story of unbelievable pain into a practical and spiritual survival kit. A great book."

JILL BRISCOE, author,
It Had to Be a Monday: Personal Reflections on the Life of Job

---

"Diane Komp's interfacing of Job's tale with stories out of her life with patients is powerful. The mystery of grace in suffering takes on a human face and soul. For those who are hurting or working with hurting people—or both!—*Why Me?* is intriguing, helpful and hopeful."

LEIGHTON FORD, author, *The Power of Story*

"In this compelling investigation Dr. Komp, with surgical skill, dissects the biblical book of Job, weaving its narrative of distress and questioning into the experiences of modern-day sufferers.

LUCI SHAW, author, *God in the Dark*

WHY ME?

A DOCTOR LOOKS AT THE BOOK OF JOB

Diane M. Komp, M.D.

InterVarsity Press
Downers Grove, Illinois

Other Books by Diane M. Komp

A WINDOW TO HEAVEN: WHEN CHILDREN SEE LIFE IN DEATH

A CHILD SHALL LEAD THEM: LESSONS IN HOPE FROM CHILDREN WITH CANCER

HOPE SPRINGS FROM MENDED PLACES: IMAGES OF GRACE IN THE SHADOWS OF LIFE

IMAGES OF GRACE: A PEDIATRICIAN'S TRILOGY OF FAITH, HOPE & LOVE

BREAKFAST FOR THE HEART: MEDITATIONS TO NOURISH YOUR SOUL

BEDTIME SNACKS FOR THE SOUL: MEDITATIONS TO SWEETEN YOUR DREAMS

ANATOMY OF A LIE: THE TRUTH ABOUT LIES AND WHY GOOD PEOPLE TELL THEM

InterVarsity Press
P.O. Box 1400, Downers Grove, IL 60515-1426
World Wide Web: www.ivpress.com
E-mail: mail@ivpress.com

InterVarsity Press® is the book-publishing division of InterVarsity Christian Fellowship/USA®, a student movement active on campus at hundreds of universities, colleges and schools of nursing in the United States of America, and a member movement of the International Fellowship of Evangelical Students. For information about local and regional activities, write Public Relations Dept., InterVarsity Christian Fellowship/USA, 6400 Schroeder Rd., P.O. Box 7895, Madison, WI 53707-7895.

All Scripture quotations, unless otherwise indicated, are taken from the Holy Bible, New International Version®. NIV®. *Copyright ©1973, 1978, 1984 by International Bible Society. Used by permission of Zondervan Publishing House. All rights reserved.*

Cover photograph: Image Select/Art Resource, NY

ISBN 0-8308-2330-1

Printed in the United States of America ∞

Library of Congress Cataloging-in-Publication Data

Komp, Diane M.
　Why me? : a doctor looks at he Book of Job / Diane M. Komp.
　　p. cm.
　Includes bibliographical references.
　ISBN 0-8308-2330-1 (alk. paper)
　1. Bible. O.T. Job—Criticism, interpretation, etc. 2. Suffering—Religious aspects—Christianity. 3. Suffering—Biblical teaching. I. Title.
BS1415.52 .K65 2001
223'.106—dc21

2001024043

22 21 20 19 18 17 16 15 14 13 12 11 10 9 8 7 6 5 4 3 2 1
19 18 17 16 15 14 13 12 11 10 09 08 07 06 05 04 03 02 01

The tears of God are the meaning of history.

But mystery remains. . . .

Why does God endure his suffering?

Why does he not at once relieve his agony

by relieving ours?

Nicholas Wolterstorff,

LAMENT FOR A SON

For Markus and Antje, Leonard and Jonas,
who are learning things too wonderful
for them to have known.

CONTENTS

SECTION IV: COSMIC QUESTIONS

Preface

> We should search the Scriptures carefully . . .
> learning not merely theoretically, but by putting
> into practice what we read.
>
> PETER OF DAMASKOS, *THE PHILOKALIA, VOLUME III*
> ———————————

A magazine editor called for an interview about a book I had written on mothers.[1] In that book I had woven composite characters based on women I met through my medical practice, but I had borrowed each heroine's name from a biblical story about family life. Furthermore, I had chosen nuggets from the scriptural narratives to craft the points of conflict for these modern lives.

We chatted about Rebekah and her feuding twin sons, Jacob and Esau. The editor remembered the biblical story with the fondness only a childhood memory could evoke. The warmth of his reaction was so hearty that I could imagine his parents reading it to him as a bedtime story. But my modern parallel intrigued him as well, a tale of dangerous sibling rivalry relevant to him as the parent of young children. My "Becky" brought the Bible's Rebekah alive for him in a fresh new way. The principle belonged to Scripture, but the story belonged to the world in which he lives.

"Then what you are saying is that the Bible really is true!" he synopsized with verve in his voice. "If that's what you think I am saying," I confirmed, "you are quoting me correctly." By the time you finish *Why Me?* I hope that you will have drawn a similar conclusion about *Job*.

The *Book of Job* is such a true story that it speaks volumes to the world in which we live. In fact Job's story has shaped my professional life. Sometimes it is Job himself—the victim—whom I meet at the hospital. Equally often it is a sufferer's family I'm called upon to help struggle through their share of losses. Why are these decent people being tormented? Why must a family face seemingly unanswerable questions? And where is God in this picture?

For thirty-five years—many as an unbeliever, more recently as a Christian—I have asked myself similar questions. Why Job? Why my friends and relatives? Why my precious little patients? Through their stories I have learned that the old adage "There are no atheists in foxholes" is sometimes true, not because those under fire bargain disingenuously with the Almighty, but because there are so many Job moments for those who are truly honest with God.

William Safire calls *Job* "the only biblical book held in reverence like a hot potato."[2] The story may be highly nourishing, but we may be more tempted to pass its message on to others who are hungry rather than to grab hold of it for ourselves. Hot or not, it's time for you and me to make a meal out of *Job's* sizzling spuds.

The *Book of Job* reads like a lyrical drama whose words evoke images of its characters and scenes. The inspired storyteller describes ideas and feelings with poetic passion but offers no tangible descriptions to complement the powerful personalities we encounter. We do not learn whether Job had a full crop of hair or was balding. We have no idea whether his eyes were brown or hazel, green or blue. Perhaps—just perhaps—the divine dramatist deliberately left the characters featureless so that you and I could sketch ourselves into the story and see our own faces reflected in Job's.

God and Satan enter into an agreement to test the faithfulness of earth's most blameless citizen. God, however, limits the extent of Job's trials. When he passes the first challenge without cursing the Almighty, the Evil One goes back to heaven and asks for more power. God allows Satan to proceed against Job's body, but he will not let him make a move against the innocent sufferer's life. A miserable man with a wretched ailment, Job sits scratching. Unaware of the dialogue about him in heaven that preceded his calamities, Job doesn't understand why all this is happening. *Why me?* he ponders.

Before you start reading *Why Me?* I suggest that you first read through the *Book of Job*. Perhaps you have never read through all forty-two chapters before. Keep *Job* open beside you as you read *Why Me?* If time permits, read it aloud to yourself as you would any dramatic work. Get into Job's act. Some parts of the book are so troubling that it's tempting to skip over them and search out more comforting passages. If you want, you can find that sort of easy comfort, but then you would not have read most of the book, and you would not have been as honest as Job.

Some of you are reading *Why Me?* because you are living through a Job-like experience right now. Others are reading this book because you hope to help hurting people. *Job* rarely becomes animated for us before we have a personal encounter with suffering. The more innocent the victim, the more we struggle with *Job's* premise. Why, with all the treacherous people in the world who deserve divine discipline, did God single out innocent Job?

Come up close to someone who is suffering if you want to understand Job. In the final weeks of her father's life, a friend listened to her Papa talk about heaven. "The first thing I want to do," he said with a smile, "is to find Job and give him a big hug." He didn't say that he wanted to "find Job and ask him some tough questions," or "find Job and compare notes with him." By virtue of his journey, Papa knew something about Job that only a fellow sufferer could fully appreciate. *Why Me?* is my invitation to you to come close enough to embrace Job.

May these stories of modern Jobs comfort and enlighten you if you are in pain, support and sustain you if you minister to those who suffer.

May the God of peace set you apart for himself through and through. May your whole spirit, soul and body be kept as blameless as Job's at the coming of our Lord Jesus Christ. The God who comforts and enlightens us, the Holy One who supports and sustains us, he is faithful. And he will do all of that! (1 Thessalonians 5:23-24, author's adaptation)

Prologue

JOB'S REGULAR CUSTOM

JOB 1:1-5

After I read . . . *To Kill a Mockingbird* . . . I knew that I wanted
to be a father like Atticus. I too wanted to be the type of man
who would stay up all night with his son or daughter
when he or she was in need.

CHRISTOPHER DE VINCK, *POWER OF THE POWERLESS*

Goodness knows that it is easier to break a child than
to mend one. So Goodness handles with care.

MIKE & AMY NAPPA, *A HEART LIKE HIS*

Picture a God-fearing, evil-shunning, upright, blameless
man. This devout rarity named Job is prosperous. Like a tax accountant our narrator ticks off Job's personal effects: sheep,
camels, oxen, donkeys, servants. Lastly, the inspired scribe notes
Job's most prized possessions: seven sons and three daughters.
Our protagonist is truly a wealthy man.

By the time we meet them, Job's children have already grown
up. A close-knit and hospitable sibship, each son has a separate
home and time enough out of a busy life to entertain his sisters
and brothers. But the partying proclivity of his offspring concerns Job. What indiscretions might his children commit during

their feasting, drinking and merriment? Above all else Job worries that in an unguarded moment his children might curse God in their hearts. Job, on the other hand, is always on guard. As Gustavo Gutiérrez notes,[1] speaking ill or speaking well of God is a central theme of the *Book of Job*. How his children speak about God is important to their father.

Please note that our narrator does *not* tell us that their sons and daughters invite Mr. and Mrs. Job to their dinner parties. As the banqueting begins, we do not hear the son hosting the evening say, "Pop, will you ask the blessing, please?" Cloistered in his own home, Job prays for his children. He even disburses from his personal wealth on their spiritual behalf. Each party costs dad ten sacrificial animals—a separate burnt offering for each son and every daughter. Just in case. *Who knows what young people do at these parties today?* thought Job. This was his regular custom.

Since we meet Job during his middle-aged maturity, we do not have the opportunity to examine his life as a young man the same age as his partying progeny. When his story begins, we learn about Job's virtues. But has Job been so upright since the day he was born?

Like Hannah, did Job's mother pray him straight from the nursery into the house of God (1 Samuel 1:28)? Or did Job party under his parents' pious noses as Eli's sons did a chapter later in Samuel's story (1 Samuel 2:12)? Job may suspect what happens at his kids' soirees because he has been there and done that himself. The scriptural storyteller does not leave this as total mystery for our imagination. In his complaint to God, Job himself hints at his early indiscretions: "You . . . hold me accountable for the sins of my youth" (13:26 The Message).

When I was growing up, my parents had friends with two

daughters close to my age. During the second World War, the father of that family served in the United States Navy. Fred* had the predictable number of sailor stories left over from that experience, but that was in the past. As an adult he became a man of active faith. When his daughters reached their teen years and had their first party at the family home, Fred was distraught. There were boys in the living room laughing and joking with *his* daughters! From personal experience he knew what pubertal boys are like. Fred's wife, Lucy, tried to keep him in the kitchen, but she could not restrain her nervous husband. When personal adolescent memories overwhelmed him, he burst into the living room, wedging himself between his daughters and their pimpled male admirers. "Pizza, anyone?" Fred bellowed. His daughters (and wife) rolled their eyes knowingly because they had heard his old sailor stories many times over.

We may not be able to go to our children's parties with them, but we can spend those hours in prayer with God. Instead of imposing our pizza or projecting our past errors onto our children, we can offer a sweet-smelling sacrifice on their behalf. To stand before God on behalf of our children is far more effective than lecturing them. Job knew this, and so he had his regular custom.

This prologue of parental concern sets the stage for the events that will follow. In it we sense the rhythm of Job's spiritual life. Not just "me and my God," but "my family and our God." All

---

*Names and minor details have sometimes been changed to maintain confidentiality and protect privacy.

is well in the land of Uz, one would think, and likely to remain so if there is any link between faithfulness and prosperity. But there is more to the universe than sleepy little Uz, tit-for-tat justice and parental concern for children. A celestial caucus is about to convene that will change all those preconceptions.

Thoughts for Modern Jobs:

1. All of us are like the Job of the Bible in that we encounter suffering and struggle to understand it. At what times have you felt in some way like Job?

2. Why do you think the storyteller includes this particular vignette at the beginning of the narrative?

3. How do you think you will pass on to your children the lessons you learned from your own youthful indiscretions? How can we separate the guilt we feel about our past blunders from our need to effectively communicate values to our children?

Thoughts for Job's Caregivers:

1. Who is the "Job" in your practice, ministry, family or circle of friends whom you want to help physically, emotionally or spiritually?

2. What do you know about your Job's relationship with family, friends and God?

3. Are all members of your Job's support network on the same page spiritually, or do they dance to different divine drummers? How does that affect the way your Job responds to suffering?

SECTION I

CONSIDER MY SERVANT JOB

It is worth noting that suffering
only becomes a problem when
we accept the existence of God.

DAVID WATSON, *FEAR NO EVIL*

1

ENTER THE ACCUSER

JOB 1:6-12

It is a terrible choice: the purifying fire of the Creator
or the deathly cold fire of Satan.

MADELEINE L'ENGLE, *TWO PART INVENTION*

Mefistophele is the embodiment of the everlasting "No!"
addressed to the True, the Beautiful, the Good.

ARRIGO BOITO, COMPOSER AND LIBRETTIST OF *MEFISTOPHELE*

Unlike other musical works that draw upon the Faust legend, Boito's opera *Mefistophele*[1] focuses on the person and work of Satan. But there is another literary work besides Goethe's masterpiece that threads its way through *Mefistophele's* libretto, one that the average music lover may not recognize. The composer borrows from the *Book of Job*.

Ave, Signor degli angeli e dei santi! As the curtain opens, a celestial choir greets the Lord God of angels and of saints. In pure and ascending tones we hear what it must have been like that day in heaven when the angels came to present themselves before the Lord (1:6). As their holy song soars to an ethereal crescendo, we hear an impudent motif intrude from somewhere deep in the bowels of the orchestra pit. The Accuser has returned from roaming back and forth on the earth (1:7).

As he springs onto the stage, Mefistophele addresses God: "Forgive me if my lowly idiom is not wholly on par with heavenly cantatas."[2] (Mefistophele's role requires a trimmer figure than that possessed by your typical operatic basso. There will be many more bounding leaps required of him before the final curtain falls.) The angels fade away, and the Evil One takes center stage. Of this you can be certain—there will be hell to pay on earth.

Like Boito's Mefistophele, Job's accuser piles on frequent-flyer miles of evil when he goes after a good man. But why is all this happening? We start asking "why?" long before the question enters the minds of Job and his friends. Neither do we like the answer that in our bones we feel is coming. From our seats in the audience we want to holler out to God on stage, "Don't ask Satan the question!" But God does ask, and we despair as we hear him say to Satan, "Have you considered my servant Job?"

"Oh, dear God," we cry out on the poor victim's behalf, "please don't pick Job!" If this could happen to Job (who does not deserve a round trip to hell and back), it surely could happen to any of us (who deserve a one-way ticket).

Satan ratchets up the pressure of his accusations. Job, he contends, bases his fear of the Lord solely on his God-given prosperity. Confident in the allure of wealth, Satan proposes that God withdraw all the wealth he has placed in Job's hands. God agrees and our hearts sink. Bad things start happening to everything that belongs to that good person. And later things will only get worse.

My job as a doctor is to take care of families like Job's. Specifically, I treat children with cancer, the most poignant of innocent sufferers. Sometimes in their hospital rooms I find their parents reading the Bible. Many of these moms and dads have never read the Bible before, but during this hellacious pilgrimage they find the *Book of Job*. Why, with all the gentle and comforting words of Scripture, do those who suffer seek out the toughest book in the Bible? Even nonbelievers turn to its pages.

Not until we experience personal suffering can we finally grasp that evil things can and do happen to people who live decent lives. They even happen to people who love and serve God.

Rachel's son and Christine's daughter were hospitalized within days of each other. The two mothers learned that they had more in common than parenting a child with cancer. Rachel was an observant Jew who raised her children to love God. Christine was an ordained minister of the Christian gospel. Each woman was shocked when her child became fatally ill. In a hidden place of their hearts each had somehow believed that her faithfulness to God had built a hedge around her children. *God, doesn't the rain fall only on the unjust?*

Unlike Job, most of us can catalogue enough sins to come up with what seems to be a pretty logical answer to "Why me?" Most of us can root out some ancient transgression for which we've never forgiven ourselves and conclude that God could never forgive us for what we've done. I hear that so often from parents in my practice. But the story of Job has little to do with that sort of human logic. That day in heaven that old liar Satan was telling the truth. It is God, not us, who builds and maintains household hedges (1:9).

Like Rachel and Christine, most of us harbor one answer to

that question in our heads and quite another response in our hearts. Not all moms and dads I meet are as aware as these two women that their conversation in this situation is with God. Some parents I meet ask a more general question: "Why do children get cancer?" Although they may not recognize it, they have a query behind their question. On a deeper level they wonder, *What did I do wrong that my child got cancer?* "Why me?" is not an etiologic investigation. It is the beginning of a spiritual quest.

When Kevin's leukemia relapsed, I started to search for a bone marrow transplantation donor for him. He didn't have a brother or sister who was a match. While we waited for a matched unrelated donor to be found, precious time seemed to be wasting. Every week I had to face his dad, Anthony, and tell him that I had no further progress to report.

During that tormenting wait, Kevin's medical status was not the only thing that was undergoing change. When I first met Anthony, he wore a small gold cross tucked under his shirt. After Kevin relapsed, that cross came out on top of his shirt where all could see it. Soon Anthony replaced it with a larger cross that bore a suffering Savior. At one particularly tense visit when I could report no progress in the donor search, Anthony kicked a waste paper basket across the room. Embarrassed by his loss of control, the mortified man apologized. "What kind of terms are you and God on these days?" I asked him. Stunned by my question, Anthony replied, "Wow, you really went to the heart of the matter!"

Inevitably, personal suffering goes to the heart of the matter: our relationship with God. If we think long enough about the root of our distress, we, like Anthony, may want to kick God clear across the room! Especially when the attack is not against ourselves but against someone we love as dearly as our children. Just how do we feel about God when he tells the hater of Job's soul, "Go ahead—do what you want with all that is his. Just don't hurt him" (1:12 The Message)? The Lord, the one who gave Job everything he has, takes back Job's possessions and hands them over to the enemy. Except for Job himself, Satan has achieved everything he wanted. But he'll be back for Job later. Exit the Accuser, stage left.

Where is that angel choir when you seem to need them most?

Thoughts for Modern Jobs:

1. What "Why me?" experience have you had in your life, a time when you couldn't believe that God was allowing something to happen to you?

2. What new thing did you learn about God during your "Why me?" experience?

3. From your own experience, what comfort would you offer a friend whose life had been touched by pure evil?

Thoughts for Job's Caregivers:

1. How has your Job expressed any "Why me?" thoughts to you?

2. What does "Why me?" have to do with your Job's spiritual journey?

3. What language does your Job use to discuss evil in the world—an impersonal force or a personal devil?

2

DISASTER HEAPED
ON DISASTER

JOB 1:13-22

Oh, there's always someone playing Job . . .
Sleeping the wrong night wrong city—
London, Dresden, Hiroshima.

ARCHIBALD MACLEISH, *J. B.*

And when I could no longer look, I blest his Name
that gave and took, That layd my goods now in the dust:
Yea so it was, and so 'twas just. It was his own:
it was not mine; Far be it that I should repine.

ANNE BRADSTREET, *SOME VERSES UPON THE BURNING OF OUR HOUSE*
JULY 10, 1666

J ust how much adversity do you think you could handle in one short day? How many tragedies do you think you could endure in a whole lifetime? Job had four large losses in one day. I remember one day at the hospital when I had four disasters heaped one on top of the other. That day I felt as if I knew what Job was going through.

Before daybreak a little boy died. As sad as Andrew's death

was, his parting came as no surprise. A nurse called me at home when his heart rate changed abruptly. I vetoed the notion of a quick shower and sped the fifteen miles to the hospital, arriving half an hour before Andrew passed away.

Andrew's parents had prepared for his death. As they surrounded his bed to say the Lord's Prayer together, they extended their hands to include me in their family circle. As was their custom, we recited the version of the prayer that ends "deliver us from the Evil One." Their son sighed and went to heaven. Family and medical staff, we hugged each other and expressed our relief that God had granted Andrew a peaceful death. I stayed with them until they needed to be alone with their child, then joined my ward team in our curtained-off conference room.

As a team we sipped coffee and reviewed the details of Andrew's final hours. We postmortemed the adequacy of our medical plan for his comfort. It had been a good plan, we all agreed. We were sad but pleased. I listened as each team member shared a personal vignette about this patient whom we all adored.

With tears in her eyes, the child's intern told of an event earlier in the evening when Andrew had called for her to come in from home on her night off. "I wanted to say 'thank you,'" Andrew said to her. As she left his hospital room this young doctor said "goodnight" but Andrew said "goodbye."

I reached across the conference table to grasp the storyteller's hand. *What a gracious gift!* I marveled. Andrew's loving gesture will follow this woman all of her days. In one brief moment a child had sealed tenderness into a doctor's heart and locked out the Evil One from her dealings with her patients.

After a final vow to be in touch with the family, I headed for the cafeteria for another cup of coffee to brace for the new day. It was too late to go home and freshen up now. It already was tomorrow.

On my way to the cafeteria I replayed the events of the last few hours in my head. No one welcomes the death of a child, but if children are going to die, let it be the way that Andrew had passed. Together we had faithfully attended to his comfort. His caregivers had both cared and given. His loved ones had been with him at his passing and took comfort from that fine gift to their son. *What about me?* I thought. *How comforted am I? I'm fine,* I concluded. *I'm good at this. I can handle death.*

Five minutes into my breakfast reverie, my beeper went off. The emergency room was calling because one of my patients was vomiting a massive amount of blood. "Can you come right away?" the voice demanded. I sighed, placed a lid on my coffee cup and headed around the corner.

As usual the ER scene was intense. Scrub-suited bodies darted around the sick child. A dissonant choir of voices shouted orders simultaneously. Karen's parents, whom the ER staff had pushed to the side, were glad to see me. Her blood platelets were low from relapsed leukemia and the child was swallowing blood. Mom told me the hemorrhage had started with a trickle of a nosebleed. I nodded and grabbed the phone to call the blood bank.

The situation looked more perilous than it actually was. The solution to Karen's problem would be a quick and easy platelet transfusion. From experience I knew that once those platelets were in her bloodstream, Karen would do just fine. Escaping the ER chaos, I shouted, "I'll go to the blood bank and pick up the platelets!" Fifteen minutes later Karen stopped bleeding.

My coffee was cold, but I declined the ER's bottom-of-the-pot grinds. Orange juice, I decided. That's the resuscitation fluid I need right now. Back in the cafeteria I sipped OJ and again reviewed the morning's events.

Satisfied, I noted that I had gone from one crisis to another.

Experience had been on my side. I could quickly assess the situation and hop directly to the best plan of action. *I'm good at this,* I thought. I wanted breakfast but food would have to wait because another family was waiting for me in the outpatient department.

I had made an early morning appointment with Pete's parents because we needed adequate time for a difficult conversation. Their son needed lifesaving treatment, but these divorced parents disagreed with each other on what course to follow. Pete's mother (who had custody) refused chemotherapy and wanted to take the child out of the country for an unproved alternative treatment she had heard about from a distant relative who materialized when Pete was first diagnosed. His father (who had lost custody at their divorce because of domestic violence) agreed with my plan. They both used Pete's illness to play out their still unresolved hostilities with each other.

At the conference room table I sat between mother and father. If Dad hauled off to sock Mom, he would have to go through me. But I did not want this man as an enemy. He was the only one who seemed to understand how soon Pete would die without the medical care I had recommended. The treatment I had outlined cured 90 percent of children with Pete's cancer. Without it, less than 10 percent could be expected to live.

I'm really tired, I thought. *This is not a good day to have to take on this problem.* As our social worker joined us, I excused myself and grabbed a cup of coffee from the clinic pot even though I was already well past my self-imposed caffeine limit for one day. A half-hour later Pete's mother agreed to talk to other moms whose sons had gone through the same treatment that I proposed. *Well, that's a good start,* I thought. I shook hands with both parents and shepherded them out the door.

I retreated to my office thinking that when you're brain dead, that's as good a time as any to attend to insurance forms. A thick stack of such nasties cluttered my desk. Uncharacteristically I gladly pulled the papers towards me. Then the telephone rang.

"The medical director from Nancy's insurance company is on the phone," apologized my secretary. "He's denying coverage for limb salvage surgery. The insurance will only pay for an amputation. Do you want to talk to him?" That did it! I had reached my mortal limit.

Death? Easy, even with interrupted sleep. Massive hemorrhage? Piece of cake when you know what you are doing. Family feuds? Thank God for social workers.

But "mangled care" after death *and* hemorrhage *and* feuding? No longer was I congratulating myself on how good I am at what I do. If the choice had been mine, one crisis per day—actually more like one per month or per year—would be a more suitable ration. Or how about no crises ever?

Consider poor Job's day: Two natural disasters (fire and wind) and two different invading troops (Sabeans and Chaldeans) wiped him out in one twenty-four-hour period. As a result, the "greatest man among all the people of the East" (1:3) was bankrupt and childless.

Compare poor Dr. Di's day: It was not my child who had died, nor I who had hemorrhaged, nor my parents who had feuded, nor my limb salvage surgery that the insurance company denied. But how quickly I had reached my limit and prepared to flee the scene! "Hey, God!" I prayed later that morning. "How about slowing things down to a more manageable pace?"

Why Job? What did he do to deserve what happened to him? And why me? In both our stories, Job's and mine, the cause of the disasters had nothing to do with us personally. We were not responsible for what had befallen us. All these adversities were due to circumstances beyond our control. True, Job chose to be a wealthy landowner and a parent. And I chose to be an oncologist. But we were the victims, not the perps.

Since you and I have read the *Book of Job*, we know that the mastermind of the evil that happened to Job was the Evil One. If in the midst of our suffering we fall into temptation, we can chalk it up to the devil. Or can we?

In a film cleverly titled *The Devil's Advocate*, a hotshot young attorney went to work for a man who helped him win one difficult case after another. Kevin Lomax (Keanu Reeves) may have set crooked clients free, but his blossoming reputation as a victorious advocate pleased him. The audience, but not Lomax, knew that his new employer was actually the devil.

Mentored by evil John Milton (Al Pacino), Kevin saw his marriage deteriorate, but his career marched forward. His wife, Mary Ann, became more and more unhinged just as Kevin took on the biggest case of his career. Milton was always supportive of his young protégé. While Mary Ann bordered on suicide, this sympathetic boss gave Kevin the option to turn his big case over to someone else so that he could attend to his wife's needs. Milton promised him that there would be no adverse consequences to his career if Kevin focused on his family crisis for a while.

Instead, Kevin chose to stay with the case—and Mary Ann took her life. Near the end of the film when his boss revealed his true identity, Kevin tried to blame the devil for the tragedy. But Milton reviewed the whole sequence of events and reminded him that at every crucial turning point, he had given him a choice. It was Kevin who had chosen to pursue his career, not the devil who had forced him to ignore his suffering wife.

After the heavenly rendezvous at which God and Satan discuss Job's case, we no longer see the Evil One. And, despite all the evil things that have happened to him, Job has not even looked for Satan's hand in his suffering. Nor has he blamed God for what has happened. "The LORD gave, and the LORD has taken away," Job observes. "Blessed be the name of the LORD" (1:21 NRSV).

How often have we blessed God's name after even one little mishap has trickled our way?

Thoughts for Modern Jobs:

1. Have you ever had a day you thought was from hell that you later learned was from heaven?

2. Have you ever experienced loss and wondered whether God let it happen to you as tit for tat for some past sin?

3. If you could edit out one of Job's disasters, which one would you delete? Loss of property? Loss of children? Loss of health?

Thoughts for Job's Caregivers:

1. In talking about the specific cause of personal suffering, does your Job focus more on goodness or on evil?

2. What combination of events was the worst "disaster upon disaster" that your Job has ever faced?

3. What planning can you and other caregivers do to reduce the disaster load on your Job and turn out days that are "blessing upon blessing"?

3

THE CASE OF
THE WANNABE WIDOW

JOB 2:1-10

Someone has altered the script. My lines have been changed.
I thought I was writing this play.

MADELEINE L'ENGLE

Mrs. Job is like the wife, Diffidence, in John Bunyan's
Pilgrim's Progress. She is the queen in the Castle of Giant
Despair, and through her husband, the Giant,
she urges Christian and Hopeful to kill themselves,
because they are imprisoned there.

EARL F. PALMER, *PRAYER BETWEEN FRIENDS*

Finally Satan gets his fondest wish, and Job has to pay with
his skin. Having limited experience with totally committed be-
lievers, Satan underestimates his prey. From the soles of his
painful feet to the crown of his oozing scalp, Job is in trouble.
But the afflicted man is not in as much trouble as his wife.

Mrs. Job has had enough. By the time her children and wealth
have vanished and a dreadful dermatological disease afflicted her
husband, his wife has a choice in mind for Job: assisted suicide.
Clearly, the marriage vows of their time did not include the clause
"for richer and poorer, in sickness and health."

"Curse God and die!" Mrs. Job suggests, intending to be helpful (2:9). Better, she thinks, to be a destitute widow than married to a bankrupt man with bad skin and integrity. Her life with Job had led her to expect only prosperity from God in their lives and not trouble (2:10). For his part, Job saw his wife's perspective as foolishly lopsided, morally defective.

So short are her lines in the *Book of Job* that artists, dramatists, poets and novelists beg for the privilege to flesh out Mrs. Job. Albrecht Durer sketches her soothing Job's pain with a bucket of cool water.[1] Georges de la Tour paints her looming menacingly over her pocked partner, a candle in her hand.[2] William Blake engraves her distraught, kneeling with her head in her hands.[3] In *God's Favorite,* playwright Neil Simon presents Job's wife as an endearing dingbat.[4] Robert Frost's Thyatira in *The Masque of Reason* is an early feminist concerned with witch-women's rights.[5] In *The Only Problem,* novelist Muriel Spark depicts Job's wife as a chocolate-thieving, bank-heisting terrorist who married her husband for his money.[6] And in Archibald MacLeish's Pulitzer Prize-winning play *J. B.*, the wife is the only truly sympathetic character.[7] Revealing the esteem in which he holds Job's wife, MacLeish gives Sarah the final pivotal speech of his poetic drama.

Sarah speaks of extinguished church candles and sky lights. In the darkness that follows, she encourages her husband to fire up the coals of their hearts. According to her worldview, restoration can come only through intimacy, not through integrity. Integrity is as cold and odd a game to her as the card game that God and Satan play offstage as they share a smoke. To her God-chilled soul, integrity is about as warm a concept as the smothered church candles and snuffed-out stars her love offers to replace. For Sarah it is an either-or matter. Her wiser-than-hubby offer seems to make sense, but it misses the importance of integrity.

A businessman called me after reading my book *Anatomy of a Lie.*[8] In the course of his work, Kurt had uncovered unethical corporate conduct at his firm that could cause widespread public harm if he didn't speak up. When he brought the problem to his supervisors' attention, they fired him. If, however, he agreed to sign a gag clause, the company promised to settle with him financially.

To make things most difficult for Kurt, his wife did not encourage him to take what he believed to be the only possible ethical stance. Donna was more concerned with the fate of their family than the moral issue at hand. How would they feed and clothe their children after Kurt went out to whack at his windmills? They had exhausted their family finances during the litigation, and their future seemed mortgaged to lawyers. Kurt even considered declaring bankruptcy.

To be a morally undivided person challenges our human relationships. Although Donna had a valid point about the needs of their family, Kurt's conscience prodded him to blow the whistle on a powerful corporation with limitless resources available to destroy him. Job, too, learned that integrity is neither a free nor a solitary ride.

Whether we sympathize with Job's wife or see her looming menacingly over him, he cannot tell his story without reference to her. But there is no such thing as wearing two ethical hats depending on the situation. "You shall love the Lord your God with your *whole* heart, mind and soul" applies at home, at worship and on the job. It is the *whole* that challenges people like Job and like Kurt. Like them we too yearn to be whole. Integrity helps me move from "Why me?" to "Since it is me, what am I going to do about it?" Integrity may be about me, but it is also about how I relate to the rest of the universe.

Discern, act, share—that's what we can do about it. Integrity is a matter of choice. Yale law professor Stephen Carter recommends these three simple steps to those of us who want to be whole persons, men and women of integrity.[9]

Job *discerned* that he had a choice to make. He could either go on living in a diminished state, or he could do as his wife suggested and end his life. He itched so fiercely that he had to scratch with a piece of broken pottery and rub ashes into his wounds to deaden the pain. Looking at this humiliating specimen of manhood, his wife questioned why he was still holding onto his integrity (2:9).

Job *acted* on what he had discerned. As maddening as his skin condition might be, he determined that he would not sin in what he said (2:10).

Finally, Job *shared* what he had discerned with his wife. "Shall we accept good from God, and not trouble?" (2:10).

Kurt would not classify himself as a hero, but he followed a similar course to Job. As much as he loved and respected his wife and family, he *discerned* that he had a larger responsibility than to care for his own. As painful as that choice was, he *acted* on what he discerned with the needs of all concerned in mind. Finally, Kurt *shared* the pain of being a whistle-blower with others, encouraging them to speak out when their own consciences motivated them to do so.

Whether or not Job's wife had given him good advice in the past, this time he was alone with God. And whether or not Satan was active in his world and circumstances, the matter once again distilled down to God and Job. Integrity means that we do not have to live at the whim of blind fate, bum advice or a nasty devil. "Although this world with devils filled shall threaten to undo us," persons of integrity in relationship with God and their fellow beings can choose to do what is right.

Thoughts for Modern Jobs:

1. Why do you think God did not allow Satan to take Job's life?

2. Make a list of synonyms for integrity.

3. Think about a difficult personal decision you have had to make where your integrity was at stake. How did you discern, act and share?

Thoughts for Job's Caregivers:

1. Who is the "wannabe widow" in your Job's story—the family member who wants the suffering to be over with as soon as possible? Is that family member in sync with the rest of the family?

2. Does your Job see his or her "wannabe widow" as an ally or an impediment?

3. Not all family members are at the same stage of grieving for the losses in Job's life. How can you help your Job's loved ones work with that reality?

SECTION II

WITH FRIENDS LIKE THESE, WHO NEEDS ENEMIES?

Deliver us from committees.

GOD TO JOB, IN ROBERT FROST'S
THE MASQUE OF REASON

4

EMPATHIC FAILURES

I imagined that my irregular person was unique and original
in his feelings and responses to me.
Not so. In fact, your irregular person and mine are probably
so much alike they could be twins.

JOYCE LANDORF, *IRREGULAR PEOPLE*

———————

I do not ask the wounded person how he feels, I myself
become the wounded person.

WALT WHITMAN, *SONG OF MYSELF*

———————

In the first chapter of *Job* we read about four plagues that robbed Job of his possessions and his children. The second chapter closes with the introduction of three of his next four "plagues." Their names are Eliphaz the Temanite, Bildad the Shuhite and Zophar the Naamanite. (We'll meet Elihu twenty chapters from now.) The three men called themselves friends. When you're rich you attract a lot of people who want to be your friend, and it appears that Job was no exception.

Word had spread throughout the region about Job's plight. Eliphaz, Bildad and Zophar planned together to call on him. These three men intended to bring sympathy and comfort. Instead, they became a part of our vernacular idiom. Even a biblically ignorant society like our own knows what it means to be a "Job's comforter."

In a meeting with modern Jobs—moms and dads who had lost children to cancer—I asked each bereaved parent to share the least helpful thing that anyone had ever said to try to comfort them. They immediately grasped what I was asking for, stories of well-intending friends who failed to put themselves into the sufferer's shoes. One mother shared the story of a friend who opined that God needed another angel so he took her daughter Michele to heaven. Michele's grieving mom bit her tongue rather than snap back at her friend that she needed her daughter more than God needed another angel. A dad told of a neighbor who said, "You must be so glad that Franky is with Jesus!" Frankly, there was nothing about Franky's death that made him glad. He wondered if his neighbor really meant to say, "You must be so glad that Franky is in heaven rather than hell." Well, at least the neighbor hadn't said that. As we continued around the table, everyone resonated with each scenario.

Even in a secular bereavement group like this one, theology abounded. Most of the unhelpful things that people said had religious content or overtones. All of us have friends who stick their own "Why me?" scenario into the stuff of our lives. But suffering people don't need pop theology from their friends. They need friends who will try to put themselves in their hurting shoes for just a little while.

If Job's friends were "empathic failures," how can we become empathic successes on behalf of suffering friends? First of all, we can investigate our own questions before we go to visit. If we think and pray through our own "Why him/her?" we may be able to put the question to rest before we visit the suffering one. And we can recognize that our real question would be "Why me?" if we were in the same situation. Solve that one (if you can!) before speaking.

Second, our suffering friends need our companionship. The Latin roots of companion, *cum pani,* literally mean "the one who shares bread." A warm meal is preferable to chilly words. Better to leave a refrigerator full of casseroles than a bellyful of aphorisms.

Third, we can offer our presence as a ministry. This precious gift was just what Job needed, but he didn't get to keep it for long enough. As they "sat Shiva"[1] with him for seven days, his friends held their silence. When we simply and silently enter into the suffering of another, we bring God along with us.

Finally, when we do speak, we can make "I" statements instead of "you" statements. If we are offering empathy and not just sympathy, the task is simpler.[2] One of the examples I offered above of "empathic failures" included the declaration, "*You* must be so glad . . . " But none of us really knows how a sufferer feels. We can only imagine. We do know, however, how *we* feel. Even if it means saying something totally unprofound, we can speak from personal experience. "I'm so sorry—I just don't know what to say," is not only honest, but it speaks from the heart.

I told you earlier about a typical experience in the hospital with a dying child. When Andrew died I found the "right" things to say to his parents. But those were professional words. When the cancer patient I must speak to is a personal friend, my thirty-five-plus years of professional experience go out the window. I too am at a loss for words. I never seem to find "perfect words"— perhaps because perfect words don't exist when our hearts are engaged.

More than anyone else in the world, a sufferer knows that

words fail in situations like Job's. Even Eliphaz, Bildad and Zophar appreciated that early in their visit (2:13). For seven days Job's friends wept aloud, tore their robes, sprinkled dust on their heads and held their silence because they saw the magnitude of his suffering (2:13). The problem began on day number eight when they opened their mouths.

I wonder how many of us would have held our silence that long.

Thoughts for Modern Jobs:

1. Describe an experience when someone acted as a "Job's comforter" toward you.

2. How did that encounter affect your relationship with that friend? with God?

3. Do you find silence or conversation more comforting? How have you communicated that preference to the people who care about you?

Thoughts for Job's Caregivers:

1. How would you distinguish *sympathy* from *empathy*?

2. Recall a time when you were an "empathic failure." Write a letter to that Job (you don't have to mail it!) rewording what you said at the time to say what you now would consider more appropriate words to share with that friend.

3. Practice the ministry of presence with your next Job and see how long you can go before you feel compelled to say something. If you break the silence because of discomfort, is it your Job's comfort or your own that was disturbed?

5

Job Wishes He Had Never Been Born

Job 3:1-26

It was not usually the big things, the awful atrocities,
that got at you. No, it was the daily pinpricks,
the little discourtesies,
the minute humiliations, having one's dignity
trodden underfoot.

Desmond Tutu, *No Future Without Forgiveness*

All he asked for was a bit of silence, a bit of shush
so he could concentrate. He wanted it to be perfectly quiet
and still, like the inside of an empty confessional
or the moment in the brain between thought and speech.

Zadie Smith, *White Teeth*

To Eliphaz, Bildad and Zophar's credit, they were not the ones to break the ashy silence in Uz. After seven silent days and nights, Job himself spoke first. What he feared most had fallen upon him. His greatest dread actually happened. No longer did he have peace in his life, no calm quietness to claim, no delicious rest to enjoy. Turmoil was Job's destiny. As a result, he cursed the day he was born (3:3-26):

"Let the Night perish; cursed be the Morn',

Wherein 'twas said, There is a Manchild born!
Let not the Lord regard that Day, but shrowd
Its fatal Glory in some sullen Cloud:
May the dark Shades of an eternal Night,
Exclude the least Beam of dawning Light;
Let unborn Babes, as in the Womb they lie,
If it be mention'd, give a Groan and die;
No sounds of Joy therein shall charm the Ear,
No Sun, no Moon, no twilight Stars appear,
But a thick Vale of gloomy Darkness wear.
Why did I not, when first my Mother's Womb
Discharged me thence, drop down into my Tomb?
Then had I been at quiet, and mine Eyes
Had slept and seen no Sorrow; there the Wise
And Subtle Counsellor, the Potentate,
Who for themselves built Palaces of State,
Lie hush'd in Silence; there's no Midnight cry
Caus'd by Oppression and the Tyranny
Of wicked Rulers. Here the Weary cease
From Labour, here the Pris'ner sleeps in Peace;
The Rich, the Poor, the Monarch, and the Slave,
Rest undisturb'd, and no distinction have,
Within the silent Chambers of the Grave."[1]

When I was a young doctor, I took care of a teenager who understood Job's lament. Carolyn was born with an inherited disease that would kill her before she reached her thirtieth birthday. "Why was I ever born?" she mourned at one visit. "Why didn't my parents take a test while I was still in the womb? If they had aborted me, I would never have had to suffer like this."

Carolyn's plaintive lament caught me by surprise. For most of her life, monthly blood transfusions had taken the place of her own damaged red blood cells. These transfusions had saved her life, but over the years, iron had built up from them that had damaged her heart. Eventually, in addition to the inconvenience of monthly transfusions, Carolyn needed painful nightly injections of a chemical to bind the extra iron and eliminate it from her body. These infusions under the skin hurt so intensely that many patients had refused this life-saving treatment. Carolyn had cooperated, but not without complaint.

Although I was certain that she would eventually die from her disease, Carolyn was still enjoying reasonable health at the time she lamented her birth. At least it had seemed so from my perspective. She was a charming young woman and an excellent student. Everyone who knew her adored her. Carolyn had not threatened to commit suicide. Neither did she ask me to help her end her life. Rather, when she lost her vision of a future, she questioned the value of the fifteen years she had had before her hope had fled.

In his second conversation with Satan, God held back one thing from Satan—Job's earthly survival. God allowed Satan to touch Job's body but not his life (2:6). And yet in his first monologue Job tells us that he does not fear death. What he fears (and exactly what has happened) is that suffering would take peace, quietness and rest away from him.

I can understand Job's point of view. Like him, I cherish peace, quiet and rest. I long for days like today—a glorious autumn morning that I can sit on my back deck with laptop, lap dog, downy woodpecker and tufted titmouse for company. But each of has our peace limit, our one greatest fear that could destroy our inner tranquility.

One day when I planned a house call on a teenager dying of cancer, I invited a friend to go along with me. Sharon was in seminary at the time preparing for lay ministry. I had already been in medical practice for twenty-odd years. Visiting the dying was not new for me, but it was a novel experience for this young woman. As we drove along, Sharon asked me a question.

"Di," she asked quietly and thoughtfully, "are you afraid of cancer?" I considered her question for a few moments before answering. My response was truthful, I believe. "No, not really," I said. "I don't like cancer at all, but I've learned so much from the children I care for that I think the fear has gone out of me. I hope that if I ever have cancer that I will remember the children I've cared for and draw from their strength." I remembered an incident fifteen years earlier. Fear had gripped the pit of my stomach just from my walking through the front doors of Memorial Sloan-Kettering Cancer Center in New York. But that would not happen today. I was satisfied with my answer.

"What about death, Di?" Sharon prodded, still in a soft, quiet voice. "Are you afraid of dying?" Again, I thought about her question carefully. Her probing was too important to be given a shallow answer. I thought about all of the deaths of children that I've witnessed, how often I have seen the peace of God descend as a gift at their parting. How grateful I would be for a similar experience at my own dying! "Again, no," I answered confidently, "not really." I came back to faith at the bedside of dying children. Because of their reliable witness, I believe that what Jesus said about coming again for us is really true.

Sharon didn't argue with either one of my answers, but she had prepared another possible fear for me to explore. "Di," she asked with the same seriousness she had asked about death and cancer, "what about being married to the wrong man?" My eyes widened in fear. My mouth became desert-dry. I steadied my white-knuckled fists on the steering wheel and reordered my breathing. "Now that," I admitted, "is absolutely terrifying!" If I were in a disastrous marriage, I could imagine myself saying with Job and Carolyn, "I wish I had never been born!"

I'm glad that Job was the one to break the seven days of silence. I'm happy for his friends that they were able to lock their lips for even that long. It isn't easy to visit someone who suffers greatly, especially when they question the value of their lives. But what are our other alternatives?

We can stay home, and not visit at all.

Or we can visit, and open our mouths straight off.

Or we can visit, and take our chances like Eliphaz and Bildad and Zophar.

If we break our silence, in all likelihood we may say something less than comforting. Perhaps we may say even something doltish. But that's all right. Job needed a sounding board, human ears to absorb his lament. And he needed to know that with their words, mere mortals were willing to take a chance on his behalf.

In the last chapter I told you about parents who come to bereavement groups. They understand why their friends' words miss the mark. And they forgive. They wonder if, had they been in their friends' places, they could have done any better. When we suffer, we all need sounding boards. The worst thing our friends could do is stay at home.

Thoughts for Modern Jobs:

1. What is your "peace limit"? What one thing in the world do you fear the most?

2. Up until this point in the story, God has called Job a "blameless" man. Should God blame Job for cursing the day that he was born?

3. If you ever had thoughts about ending your own life, did you tell someone or keep it to yourself? If you didn't tell anyone, why did you keep it private?

Thoughts for Job's Caregivers:

1. Describe a personal experience where you felt ill at ease ministering to a suicidal person.

2. What disturbed you most about that encounter? What was the outcome?

3. Put yourself in my place as Carolyn's caregiver and write out how you think you would respond to her desire never to have been born.

6

ON SUICIDE WATCH

JOB 4:1-7:21

Job has ostensibly sown pedigreed, high quality,
pure wheat seed, why then does he reap sorrow and anguish?
... Can the writer weasel out of this apparent dilemma
by making fine distinctions?

ROB SHELDON, *JOB AS NATURAL SCIENTIST*

One day your banged-up, bruised body
won't matter a whole lot.
Right now it screams for your undivided attention.

JONI EARECKSON TADA, *WHEN IS IT RIGHT TO DIE?*

Sleep did not come easily to Eliphaz the seven silent nights he visited with his distraught friend. In a troubling dream, a spirit glided past his face and made his body hair stand on end. In his dream Eliphaz heard a hushed voice say, "Can mortals be more righteous than God? Can a man be more pure than his Maker?" (4:17). Frightened by this apparition, Eliphaz feared for Job. He called the once blameless man to repentance: "If it were I, I would appeal to God; I would lay my cause before him" (5:8). The truth of his statement was self-evident, he felt. He admonished Job to hear his words and apply them to his situation. Clearly it was Job's desire for death that pushed Eliphaz to break his silence.

In his cautious first speech Eliphaz tells us what kind of man Job was before these calamities changed his life forever. As a teacher Job had strengthened the feeble hands and faltering knees of many others (4:3, 4). His words had encouraged those who had stumbled along life's way. But now Job is hopelessly discouraged. He flirts with death, yet death (as Eliphaz reminds him) is not for the blameless. "Who, being innocent, has ever perished?" (4:7). Should not Job's piety be his confidence, his blameless ways his hope? (4:6). In his response Job complains that he feels as if he has been placed on suicide watch (7:12).

How frightening it is to deal with a friend whose life might rest in the balance of our words! In contrast to Job's era, today we prefer to refer such cases to mental health professionals. It's their job, we tell ourselves. Therapists will know exactly the right words to say. But it doesn't always work out that way. Sometimes the words of counsel fall to a friend.

One day before I was leaving on a long trip to Germany, a friend called me at my office. I winced when my secretary told me that Nadine was on the line. I had so much to do before leaving that I didn't have time for a social phone call from a friend with serious emotional problems. But I took the call anyway and heard a hysterical Nadine speaking from what sounded like an outdoor telephone booth. "I know you're incredibly busy today," Nadine wept, "but I didn't know who else to call." *What about your therapist?* I thought, and then remembered that there was a phone booth outside her therapist's office.

On the phone Nadine told me that the session with her therapist had unleashed suicidal thoughts. I remembered a similar phone call from her the day before the last time I left the country. There seemed to be a pattern here, but what do you say to someone who tells you that they may take their life? With a full day of appointments ahead of me, I told her to come over to my office anyway. Meanwhile I was thinking, *Why me? Why has Nadine put me, who is not a qualified mental health professional, in this difficult position?* I felt unprepared to deal with a suicidal patient.

I called her therapist and asked for advice. "What do I do if she's really suicidal?" I asked frantically. "Send her to the emergency room," was the response. Well, at least my office is in the same building as the ER.

Earlier that day I had met with my regular prayer partner. Michael had met Nadine through me, and while we were praying, she came into his thoughts and heart. Now, with Nadine on her way to my office, I called Michael and asked if he was free to join us. Short minutes later, he was on his way.

When Nadine reached my office, she was anxious and falling apart. She sat obediently in the chair I pointed to and tearfully explained the events of the morning. When Michael arrived, the three of us began to pray. First I prayed out loud, although countercurrent thoughts were distracting me. *What am I doing with a suicidal woman in my office when the emergency room is only three floors below?* I asked myself. But I kept praying until Michael picked up the thread of prayer. As I listened to his calm, quiet voice, I peeked at Nadine to judge her state of mind. She was still tense, but at least she was safe sitting in that chair. Then Michael began to pray in tongues.

My first reaction was to panic. This wasn't part of Nadine's faith practice, nor was it part of mine. *Might this tip her over the edge?* I wondered. I poked Michael in the ribs, but he paid me no mind. I don't even think he felt my urgent prod. My anxiety level rose. I could imagine the scene that would follow in the emergency room, her therapist asking me, "Now, just what was going on in your office right before she decompensated?" I jabbed Michael again but he continued to pray. Cautiously I stole a glance at Nadine. Her demeanor had radically altered. The tight worry lines around her eyes had melted. Peace had transformed her face. Amazed, I sat back in my chair. When Michael finished praying, Nadine started to pray herself. She thanked God for his gift of peace and for caring friends. We all said "amen," opened our eyes and sat back.

"I'm OK now," Nadine offered with a convincing tone. "Do you want to go to the ER?" I countered. "No," she said, "don't worry. I'll be OK at home. The suicidal thoughts have passed. Thanks for making time for me on such a busy day." With a curious look on her face she turned to Michael. "What language was that you were praying in?" she asked him. She had no idea what ecstatic speech or praying in tongues was. All she knew was that while Michael was praying, the peace of God swept over her and carried her to safety.

I tell you this story not as a model for management of suicidal friends but to illustrate how anxious we become when we are on suicide watch. The answer, we think, must lie in perfect words— either our own or, better yet, those of a professional. But it doesn't always work out that way. Sometimes it falls to a friend to sit with a friend and wait for God to most unexpectedly appear.

About an hour after Nadine left my office, her therapist called me. "How is Nadine? Where is she?" she asked. "She's fine. She's at home now," I explained. "At home? What did you do? What did you say to her?" she pursued. "Oh," I answered, "we just prayed."

Back in Uz, Eliphaz was having less success with Job than we had with Nadine. His words irritated the suffering man, but Eliphaz hung in there just the same. Job claimed there was no wickedness on his lips that he knew of (6:30). With his integrity at stake, Job demanded that Eliphaz recant his words. Even if a man turned his back on God, Job said, he would still deserve the devotion of his friends (6:14).

If Job is blameless, it is not because he is sinless. Job's status before God rests on his sensitivity to and confession of his offenses. Job isn't a perfect man—he's simply a forgiven one. But God has Job on suicide watch too. "Will you never look away from me, or let me alone even for an instant?" Job says to God (7:19). He admits what God knows and his friends suspect. "I despise my life; I would not live forever. Let me alone" (7:16). Finally, Job asks God his burning questions: "Why have you made me your target? Why do you not pardon my offenses?" The question "Why?" will stalk us throughout this book.

Thoughts for Modern Jobs:

1. Do you think Job was determined to end his life, or was he simply a depressed man crying for help?

2. Would you like to live to be one hundred years old? If yes, why? If not, why not?

3. In your opinion (and in the words of a modern playwright), whose life is it anyway?

Thoughts for Job's Caregivers:

1. Has anyone ever told you that they didn't want to live any longer? How did you respond?

2. Having read *Job*, would you answer them any differently now than you did at the time?

3. In your ministry or practice, how do you deal with Jobs who talk about assisted suicide?

7

THE PROBLEM
OF ARGUMENT

JOB 8:1—10:22

> [Job] not only argued the problem of suffering,
> he suffered the problem of argument.
>
> MURIEL SPARK, *THE ONLY PROBLEM*

> Try to listen with the love of Christ,
> tasting what another is saying before you respond.
>
> EM GRIFFIN, *SCRATCHING WHERE THEY ITCH*

Have you ever had a friend who had a lot to say, but who didn't listen to you when it was your turn to speak? Job found himself in such a dilemma with his friend Bildad. Consider Bildad's accusatory statements:

> *Your* words are a blustering wind. (8:2)
> But if *you* will look to God . . . (8:5)
> If *you* are pure and upright . . . (8:6)
> How long will *you* say such things? (8:2)

From the prologue of the *Book of Job* we know that even if Bildad had followed Job's example, he could not be as pure or upright as his teacher. In regard to moral behavior, God said that no one on earth compared to Job. But this established fact did not stop Bildad from delivering a sermonette when his turn came to speak.

Bildad's may be the unkindest speech of all. Nowhere are we more vulnerable than in the matter of our children. "When *your* children sinned against him," Bildad intones, "[God] gave them over to the penalty of their sin" (8:4). He hits below the belt with his cause-and-effect theology and scores a double whammy. Bildad may not have discovered Job's secret sin, but he certainly knows about Job's kids' parties. Sitting at the gate as a teacher, Job may well have shared his parental concerns with his friends.

Good parents feel responsible for their children, and society suffers when parents fail to take their responsibilities seriously. None of us would argue with that. But is the time of suffering the appropriate time to bring these issues into conversation? The questions of "Why me?" or "Why my children?" may be universal ones, but the answers are hardly uniform.

Job may be Everyperson, but the cause of his suffering is not the same as everyone's. Nor are proximate circumstances of suffering always of theological importance. One child may die of AIDS because of needle-sharing use of drugs. Another may die of the same disease because of a blood transfusion given during surgery. One young man may die while engaging in the risky sport of bungee jumping. Another may perish as the passenger in a car that someone else was driving. Human nature says we should follow the behavior trail if we want to know why, but divine nature says we should dwell instead on the word of God.

"Rabbi, who sinned, this man or his parents that he was born blind?" asked Jesus' disciples. "Neither," he replied, "this happened so that the work of God might be displayed in his life" (John 9:2). *Why did Job's children perish?* wonders Bildad. Somebody must have sinned. For his part, Job admits that there is an element of truth in what Bildad said *if* applied to the proper situation (9:1). Since we are privy to Job's heart on the matter, we know that he has taken every proper parental precaution and confessed every personal sin. And since we were witnesses to heaven's conversation, we know that Job's children did not die because of evil behavior, their own or their parents'.

It is hard for me to read Bildad's jab at Job's children without wincing. For me, Job is every parent whose child has been my patient. Even more so, Job is every parent whose child has died a sudden and unexpected death. The little deaths of "anticipatory grieving" that I witness through cancer are an act of kindness, a liturgy of gestation. Not so when death comes swiftly and without preparation to parents like Job and his wife.

Job's experience belies the oversimplification of any neat and tidy system that "stages" grief. Rather than beginning with *Why me?*—to some the vocabulary of denial, Job starts with *Why not me?*—the language of acceptance. "Naked I came from my mother's womb, and naked I will depart. The LORD gave and the LORD has taken away" (1:21).

Bildad's words may reflect his theology of suffering, but they do not speak to Job's circumstances. We can only know what sufferers are feeling when we ask them to explain. I found myself in a similar dilemma to Bildad's when I recently followed my own train of thought rather than taking the time to determine a suffering friend's concerns.

Since the last time I had seen Sabine, she had been through painful carpal tunnel surgery. Unfortunately, she hadn't recovered the function of her hand and still suffered from the same chronic neuropathic pain that had driven her to consider surgery in the first place. I knew that this type of pain is very difficult to treat. As I listened to Sabine list all the pain relievers that her doctors had prescribed, I noted that they had tried everything reasonable. They had offered the right drugs, but poor Sabine had endured so many side effects from these medicines that she couldn't function when she took them to relieve her pain. Sabine's was not an easy case.

I wanted to be helpful, so I asked Sabine if she would like for me to pray with her. She looked at me slightly startled and said, "Sure, but I was hoping I could ask for your medical opinion." She had dozens of friends to pray with her, but I was the only friend she had with more than thirty years' experience treating such horrible pain. She was long on prayer partners and short on qualified medical experts.

Like Bildad, I had listened to my friend with my ears and drawn my own conclusions. In retrospect, I should have hearkened with my heart and asked, "What can I do to help you?" How much shorter the *Book of Job* would have been if any of his four friends had asked the poor man the same simple question!

In *The Only Problem*, Muriel Spark's novel based on *Job*, an old friend visits the Job-type, Harvey Gotham. Edward is a former pastor who has found his true calling on the stage. In retrospect, this actor who has a bit of Bildad in him must admit that what he enjoyed most about ministry was having a pulpit from which to perform. When preaching, Edward was more conscious of his delivery style than the actual sermon content. His visit to his old friend was to solve a problem, not to understand the situation from Harvey's point of view. As Spark notes, Job not only had to "argue the problem of suffering, but he suffered the problem of argument as well."[1]

When we want to support friends, we should try our hardest to place ourselves in their stead. To do that we should make "I" statements, talk about what we feel and think we can do for them. As effective empathizers—in-their-shoes friends—we can also clarify what we might not otherwise understand. Empathic dialogue is not an argument. It is as different from the series of speeches in *Job* as a communication form can be. "I understand you correctly to say . . . ?" and "Let me see if I grasped what you were saying . . . " are suitable ways to begin our conversation. And perhaps the best question of all: "What can I do to help you?"

———❧———

Late one night a physician in another city sent a teenage patient to my hospital. Fifteen-year-old Gerry knew from his symptoms that his cancer had recurred, but he didn't want to believe it. Since he and his family believed that God could heal any disease if their faith was strong enough, he chose to pray rather than report his suspicions to his doctor. Finally, a school teacher noted how pale he was and called his parents. A brief examination confirmed the relapse, and the doctor recommended treatment. When Gerry and his family refused treatment, the doctor argued with them about their religious beliefs. She threatened to report them to the child protective services if they did not agree to come to my hospital for treatment. Things were very tense on the ward when I arrived that night to see him.

Gerry's dad stood in front of his son's hospital room door with his arms folded across his chest. He grunted a brief greeting to me without changing his posture. "What can I do to help you?" I asked him.

"Help me?" he asked, incredulously. "We're here because we don't have a choice."

I guided him down the hallway to a friendly visiting room. "Of course you have a choice," I told him. "I'm not going to order any treatment you and Gerry don't want." I had no intention to ask a court to approve chemotherapy against the young man's will. "If you think treatment will help, we'll make a plan together. If you don't want treatment, you're free to go home." I watched as the father crumbled into a chair.

As long as authority figures argued with him over his life's philosophy (and theology), he was angry and defiant. But when the control was solely in his hands, he fumbled his way to the path he needed to take. "You need to do a bone marrow exam, don't you?" he asked. "That's the only way you'll know how advanced the cancer is, isn't it?"

I handed him a cup of coffee. "If you and Gerry want me to," I answered, "I'll do a bone marrow examination. But if you're not planning to go through treatment, there really isn't any point to put him through the pain of the procedure."

Dad invited me to go with him to talk to his son. "If I pray over Gerry during the bone marrow, he doesn't feel the pain. Is that all right with you?" A half-hour later we had a mutually acceptable treatment plan.

During the months that followed, Gerry's dad sat in his room with a Bible open to one of two verses: "I will not give my glory to another" (Isaiah 48:11)—glory-grabbing doctors, beware! Or, "You may ask for anything in my name, and I will do it" (John 14:14)—if I name it, God will let me claim it. I never persuaded that dad that medical care in the name of Christ glorifies God. Nor did he agree with me that because other Christians with great faith had died of cancer, that was a possibility for his son within the will of God. Neither did I try to persuade him. With time he came to understand that his argument was not with me or the medical establishment. Like Job, his argument was with God.

What would have happened if Bildad had tried to understand what Job was saying instead of matching wills with him? Perhaps

Job's emotional suffering would have been of shorter duration. But it was not for his interaction with Bildad that Job sought arbitration. He felt that Almighty God was stalking him like a lion (10:16). Job, who sought a mediator in his argument with God, could not rely on Bildad or any of his friends to help him. Rather than bearing comfort, they bore witness against him (10:17). As difficult as Job's situation was, he knew that his dialogue must be with God. "Tell me what charges you have against me" (10:2), Job prayed. He sought to understand his situation from God's point of view.

Thoughts for Modern Jobs:

1. How easy is it for you to be honest with God? How easy is it for you to be angry with God?

2. Chances are if you ever were angry with God that you showed your anger in some other way before you realized who you were really mad at. What ways did you express it? Who were your targets?

3. Have any of your friends ever felt agitated when you shared your honest feelings about God with them? Why do you think your blunt honesty upset them at the time?

Thoughts for Job's Caregivers:

1. Think about a situation where it was very difficult to listen to a troubled friend go on and on and on. Rather than judging that monologue, focus on what your Job was asking you to do on his or her behalf.

2. Practice empathic dialogue with a friend, colleague or someone you love. Pick a controversial topic that you think might be very difficult to hear the other person's point of view.

3. From your empathic dialogue session make a list of emotional trigger points that made it especially hard for you to hear what the other person was saying.

8

WORTHLESS PHYSICIANS

JOB 11:1—14:22

> To write prescriptions is easy, but to come
> to an understanding with people is hard.
>
> FRANZ KAFKA, *A COUNTRY DOCTOR*

> They were worthless physicians, who neither understood
> [Job's] case nor knew how to prescribe to him—
> mere empirics, who pretended to great things,
> but in conference added nothing to him:
> he was never the wiser for all they said.
>
> MATTHEW HENRY, *COMMENTARY ON THE WHOLE BIBLE*

We have high expectations from the words of our trusted friends. We have reason to believe that those who are closest to us and care about our welfare are in the best position to perceive our needs. When they care, we take on strength. Not so for Job and his friends. Eliphaz, the first to speak, started out on a cautious tone. Zophar was not so discreet. When his turn came, Zophar hurled insults at the stricken man:

Is this *talker* to be vindicated? (11:2 NIVI)
Should your *idle talk* reduce others to silence? (11:3 NIVI)
Will no one rebuke you when you *mock?*"(11:3 NIVI)
But the *witless* can no more become wise. (11:12 NIVI)

Not as stupid as Zophar alleged, Job replied in kind:

> I have a mind as well as you. (12:3 NIVI)
> Those who are at ease have contempt for misfortune. (12:5 NIVI)
> If only you would be altogether silent! For you that would be wisdom. (13:5 NIVI)
> You are worthless physicians, all of you! (13:4 NIVI)

〜〜✲〜〜

As a doctor I wince when I hear Job indict his helpers as "worthless physicians." Admittedly it is hard to be around a depressed person, to be the "worthwhile physician" they need. How frightening to think about a friend possibly committing suicide! And how absolutely horrifying to hear someone be as honest with God as Job was. How much easier it is to physically, emotionally and verbally place distance between ourselves and that person. But some of the most healing moments for the Jobs of this world come when those who care step back from our list of professional expectations and put ourselves in the place of the one who is hurting.

On a tragic weekend one of my patients died under mysterious circumstances. Compounding his parents' grief was the obligatory involvement of the medical examiner to review the case. Rather than fulfilling the all-too-deserved stereotype of his profession, this medical examiner anticipated the extra burden that his involvement would cause the family. He called them at home and assured them that his intention was to help. He visited them in the funeral home and extended his personal condolences.

Why did this particular medical examiner practice "business as unusual"? Not only is he a warm-hearted man, but he is the father of two sons close to the dead boy's age. The doctor put himself into the family's shoes, pouring out his empathy. Rather than destroying his objectivity, he was more effective in carrying out his medical duties than if he had kept the usual professional distance expected of his trade. For the boy's parents he became a worth*while* physician of the sort that Job hoped for.

Although Job's comforters talked a lot *about* God, we have scant indication that they talked *to* God. But is prayer the role of a physician? Dr. Larry Dossey uses scientific studies to prove that it is. Although Dossey had set aside the religious beliefs of his childhood, he couldn't escape the observation that patients do better when their doctors pray for them. "A simple attitude of prayerfulness, an all-pervading sense of holiness and a feeling of empathy, caring, and compassion . . . seemed to set the stage for healing."[1]

Patients afflicted with wounds, headaches and anxieties—injuries like Job's—did better from a simple prayer like "Thy will be done" than from more specific requests for explicit healing such as Gerry's dad had prayed (chapter seven). Despite Dossey's biases against religion, the doctor had to conclude that to *not* pray would be equivalent to withholding a known effective remedy from his patients.

As John Mark Hicks learned, prayer requires honesty with God. After the death of his wife to cancer and his only son to a rare genetic disease, he recognized prayer as an important clue to how we interpret God's involvement in the world.[2]

Most of us would rather embrace a triumphal view of a faith-filled life and hear sufferers holler "Hallelujah!" than let them be honest with their Maker. That's what happened to a young doctor who asked for my help with a patient.

Although the doctor wasn't a Christian, he was very attached to a teenage patient who was. When Greg's death approached, the doctor expected the boy's Christian faith to carry him through buoyantly. Greg might suffer in body, but not in the spirit. At least that was the doctor's assumption. Near the end of his life, Greg took his doctor by surprise by telling him that he was afraid to die. *A Christian afraid of death?* That wasn't the way the doctor had expected it to be! Greg would be with Jesus soon. That was the boy's firm belief and a support that his doctor had counted on. He wanted Greg's death to be a spiritual victory. I suppose we could call that (and Zophar's) viewpoint "triumphalism by proxy."

At the doctor's request, I went with him to talk to his young patient. In recent weeks Greg had suffered terrible nosebleeds that were hard to stop. When his doctor offered hospice home care as an alternative to hospitalization, Greg became distraught. Instead of seeing the offer as compassionate, he perceived it as abandonment. I asked him what it was about death that he feared most. "I don't know what will happen to my mother after I die," he confided.

His mother was a widow who had worked hard to maintain health insurance for him during his illness. What would her life be like without him? With Greg's permission, I shared his fears with his mom. This gracious woman embraced her son and told him in concrete terms why she knew she would be okay after his death. And then she prayed for her son.

Like Job's friends, we reach for words to try to comfort the suffering, yet panic when they are truly honest with God about their distress. But the sick and suffering need those honest words with God for their healing to begin. When someone is enduring a torturous illness, it is fiendishly hard to find the simple words "Thy will be done." When someone is lacking peace (depressed), we want them to feel better. We may fear that God's will for someone like Greg or Job may not be the healing of their physical afflictions. Apparently God's will for Greg did not include healing of his cancer. But God did will that Greg be at peace about his mother. Miraculously, when that peace came the bleeding stopped. She became his most worthwhile physician.

When sufferers are honest with God, don't be embarrassed when they express anger. Don't share your dreams with them as Eliphaz did. Listen to theirs. Be honest with God yourself. And most of all, pray for those who suffer in body and spirit. Dip in the deep, healing well of "Thy will be done." Your prayer will help you support others who need to do the same.

Thoughts for Moderns Jobs:

1. Make a list of ten attributes you think would constitute a "worthwhile physician."

2. Think of a personal problem about which you need to be more honest. How do you think your friends would react if you told them the God-honest truth?

3. In what area of your life do you need to say to God, "Thy will be done"?

Thought for Job's Caregivers:

1. Make a list of ten things you would like to change about yourself to make you a more "worthwhile physician."

2. Which of these changes do you think you're most likely to accomplish? least likely?

3. How can the words "Thy will be done" heal a wounded healer?

SECTION III

WITNESSES FOR
THE PROSECUTION

When discipline of the tongue is
practiced . . . each individual will . . .
cease from constantly scrutinizing
the other person, judging him,
condemning him, putting him in his
particular place where he can gain
ascendancy over him and thus doing
violence to him as a person.

DIETRICH BONHOEFFER, *LIFE TOGETHER*

9

EMPTY NOTIONS

JOB 15:1—17:16

The endless cycle of idea and action,
Endless invention, endless experiment,
Brings knowledge of motion,
     but not of stillness;
Knowledge of speech, but not of silence;
Knowledge of words, and ignorance of the Word . . .
Where is the Life we have lost in living?
Where is the wisdom we have lost in knowledge?

T. S. ELIOT, *CHORUSES FROM "THE ROCK"*

If knowing answers to life's questions is absolutely necessary
to you, then forget the journey.

MADAME JEANNE GUYON

Have you ever been in a word war that heats up so fast you feel like yelling "Time out!" to recover perspective? Starting with Zophar's first monologue (11:1-20), Uz became that sort of windy hot spot. In their second round of speeches Job's other friends turned up the heat as well. Eliphaz, who had been cautious in his first speech, now disputed Job's worldview. Considering everything they had seen and heard, his friends should have been on his defense team. Instead they became witnesses for the prosecution.

Their major indictment against Job was that by sticking to his claim of innocence, he threatened sound religion. Although Job once was his favorite spiritual mentor, Eliphaz now fears that Job will turn others away from fearing God and following his ways (15:4). He assaults the suffering man as a hapless heretic.

In the first cycle of speeches Job's friends groped in the dark to unearth his unconfessed sin. This time around they think they are onto something. Anyone who makes the claims that Job makes must have hidden blameworthy thoughts behind them. Eliphaz builds his case by focusing on the organs of speech:

> For sin prompts your *mouth*. (15:5)
> You adopt the *tongue* of the crafty. (15:5)
> Your own *mouth* condemns you, not mine. (15:6)
> Your own *lips* testify against you. (15:6)

But why should Eliphaz be Job's new teacher? What does his worldview express that corrects Job's?

We can't discuss the *Book of Job* without making reference to the most popular modern work on innocent suffering that makes reference to Job. I read Rabbi Harold Kushner's bestselling *When Bad Things Happen to Good People*[1] shortly after it was released. Although the author did not share my personal interpretation of *Job*, I shared his book with Jewish families in my medical practice thinking that they might find it useful.

Like these families, Rabbi Kushner's personal initiation to the world of Job was through the illness of his child. With King David's words on the death of his and Bathsheba's first child (2 Samuel 12:22-23), Kushner dedicated his book (which has become a modern classic) to the memory of his son. Aaron Zev Kushner died of progeria[2] at age fourteen. The families with whom I shared the book appreciated Kushner's status as a fellow pilgrim, but one father described his reaction to the book in the language of *Job*. "He speaks empty notions full of hot east wind" (15:2). Others said that Kushner states the problem but doesn't offer a solution. To these parents Kushner was as useful as one of Job's comforters. His motivation was beyond reproach but, in their opinion, he missed the point and left them feeling empty.

Rabbi Kushner believed he was telling the truth. But each of us must discern carefully between truth-telling and a mere presentation of our own point of view. Without revelation, truth is just as unknowable as postmodern thinkers claim it to be. Without divine revelation, different points of view are all that we have. We cannot simply go our separate ways (as respectful or tolerant as we may be) and agree to disagree without searching for a common (truth-filled) ground.

Moses Maimonides, an outstanding medieval Jewish scholar, saw different worldviews on Providence popular in his time expressed by Job and each of his friends.[3] Without God's explanation of the series of events in Job's life, who is to say which of the five worldviews expressed is the right one? Postmodernists thumbing through *Job* might see exactly what they would have predicted: five human beings with five different versions of the truth.

In the final year of my father's life, my sister and I made many long-distance trips to visit him in a nursing home in a state where neither of us lived. Marge and I had not lived under the same roof for nearly forty years. Many of our visits back home had been at separate times, but in the last few months of Dad's life we planned to be there together. There were important decisions for us to make on which we needed to find agreement.

Dad, who already suffered from the effects of a stroke and dementia, now had terminal cancer. Since he had been out of circulation for a number of years, we wondered what to do about his funeral. We considered the option of a simple graveside commitment rather than a full service. What would happen if we had a service but no one came? But there was a "revelation" that covered the matter.

On my bulletin board at home was a 3" x 5" card written some years earlier in the hand of my very practical stepmother. The card contained the name and phone number of their lawyer, the cemetery name and location of their prepaid burial plots, the location of their safety deposit boxes, the location of their wills and a very clear message: "Your father and I both want a memorial service in our church rather than in a funeral home."

I stayed up all night planning a memorial service in the church that my father loved. "Where will I find a soprano on such short notice who knows those songs?" asked the brand new pastor, whom I had never met. (I was relieved to hear that he had faithfully visited my dad in the nursing home. Several times I had asked Dad if the pastor was visiting. He always said, "Oh yeah!" If I asked Dad which of the three pastors, he couldn't find the name but he would say "the head guy." Since I spent my Sundays with Dad, I didn't know that the "head guy" and two "next-to-head-guys" whom I used to know had been gone from that church for at least two years!)

The pastor found an organist who could play all the Bach pieces I had asked for and a soprano who wondered why he thought she wouldn't know Leonard Bernstein's "Simple Song" and "Brother James Air." Wisely the pastor suggested that Marge and I hold a reception line before the service to greet the people who came. One church member who knew my father's passion for classical sacred music told the pastor that he would arrange to tape the service. He knew that Richard Komp's daughters would plan a service filled with music. The Hammond Organ Society was there in full force, even though Dad hadn't been to a meeting in more than ten years. A remarkable number of old friends were there as well.

Without revelation all we have are empty notions, our own points of view. The more we hear from Job's friends, the more we want to hear from God instead. And so does Job. When the prosecution has rested and the defense puts on its case, there is only one witness whom Job plans to call. "My witness is in heaven, and he that vouches for me is on high" (16:19).

Thoughts for Modern Jobs:

1. What in your life do you consider unjust?

2. If you had the opportunity to take your case to court, whom would you call as your witnesses?

3. What things are so important to you that you'd like to make sure your loved ones know how to carry out your wishes? How could you communicate that to them so that there can be no mistake what you wanted?

Thoughts for Job's Caregivers:

1. Describe a time when you tried to help a Job but got into deeper misunderstanding every time you opened your mouth.

2. Why do you think the misunderstanding happened?

3. Revisit that experience and write out an empathic dialogue that might better minister to that situation.

10

UNFAVORED MERIT

JOB 18:1—19:29

In trying to make stories "work," I have discovered . . .
frequently it is an action in which the devil has been
the unwilling instrument of grace.

FLANNERY O'CONNOR, *MYSTERY AND MANNERS*

Anyone who writes about grace
must confront its apparent loopholes.

PHILIP YANCEY, *WHAT'S SO AMAZING ABOUT GRACE?*

In his final hour on the cross Jesus taught a remarkable lesson about grace (Luke 23:39-43). One of the criminals who was crucified with him challenged him (if he really was the Messiah) to save himself and the two of them hanging beside him. The other criminal saw justice in their death sentences: "We are punished justly for we are getting what our deeds deserve" (Luke 23:40). Tenderly, this second criminal turned to Jesus—whom he recognized to be innocent—and asked Jesus to remember him when he came into his kingdom. In response, Jesus told the late-repenting criminal that he would be with him in paradise on that same day.

A classical case of grace—unmerited favor instead of justice. But the thief on the cross created a dilemma for those of us who turn to faith early in our lives the way Job had. Even if a childhood experience of faith leads to a long and virtuous new life, the dying thief is our equal (and Job's) in the economy of grace.

As Handel noted in his beloved aria "I Know That My Redeemer Liveth," Job's plight prefigured the Messiah. Job spoke of a Redeemer who would stand on the earth at end times (19:25). In fact, Job's heart yearned to see this Advocate who would speak out on his behalf. Like the dying thief, Job expected justice. Unlike the dying thief, Job wished to make a case for his innocence. It was not grace Job sought but justification. But it was grace he received—unfavored merit—just the same. There are two sides to the coin of grace.

The word *grace* does not appear as such in the *Book of Job*, but its fingerprints are detectable throughout. Frankly, it's easier to understand and yearn for grace when you are not blameless. The crucified thief knew better than to ask for justice. Job, on the other hand, had lived a repent-as-you-err life. So sensitive was Job to sin that he resisted it or repented from it at every turn. To the best of his ability he had lived by God's law as he knew it.

Job was not a perfect man but a forgiven one. He was a man as much in need of grace as the penitent thief—and you and me. This law-abiding man was not looking for grace. He preferred justice and wanted favor for his merit. But grace, not justice, was the greatest gift that Job would ever receive.

Although he was not looking for grace directly, Job's quest for a Redeemer opened his heart to the reality that his good works were not enough. "The law," as Paul notes, "was added so that the trespass might increase. But where sin increased, grace increased all the more, so that, just as sin reigned in death, so also grace might reign through righteousness to bring eternal life through Jesus Christ our Lord" (Romans 5:20-21). Even blameless Job needed to be amazed by grace.

I wonder what thoughts Job might have pondered if his friends had not come to visit? If his friends had all deserted him like his kin, guests, servants, wife and even the little village boys (19:14-15), what would he have imagined? Rather than being surrounded by icons of his past, Job would have been alone with his thoughts and alone with God. But he needed a human audience for his words, and so do we. Whether on a cross or an ash heap, grace doesn't happen in a vacuum.

In Neil Simon's play *God's Favorite*,[1] Joe Benjamin (who typifies Job) suffers through one loss after another. We see his body afflicted and bandaged. His skin is so tender that he cannot accept a kiss from his daughter without excruciating pain. Distracted by his torment, Joe suffers one challenge to his faith after another. Physically he is a pitiful sight. His wife finds his breath offensive and mocks his abiding relationship with God. "He's my God and I love him!" Joe cries out. Jealous of her husband's tight relationship with God, Rose yearns wistfully, "Why can't you just have a mistress like other men?" Joe hears many seductive voices that invite him to denounce God. One voice appears to be the voice of God himself. Despite Joe's preoccupation with his horrible skin and his miserable mouth, his affliction does not distract him so much that he believes this blasphemy.

Notwithstanding accusations that his ideas are empty notions, Job knows the difference between God's concepts and those of somebody else. In the moments when he feels most deserted Job cries out, "Oh, that my words were recorded, that they were written on a scroll, that they were inscribed with an iron tool on lead, or engraved in rock forever!" (19:23-24). He wishes for immortality, or at least that his words be recorded to show that he is blameless. *Forever!* But in his assurance of blamelessness, Job leaps by faith to the belief that long after skin worms destroy his body he will see God (19:26). This heart-yearning, rock-engraving, grace-enabling plea is so strong that Job confidently believes that he will see God with his own eyes (19:27).

Although he doesn't recognize the nature of his staying power, by the grace of God Job hangs in there believing in his final vindication. As the dying thief learned, that form of firm faith opens the floodgates of grace. Faith, taught Karl Barth, occurs when I hold fast in spite of all that contradicts faith.[2] Job holds fast and will not renounce God. He wants to stand face to face with God so he can ask his burning question, "Why me?" By the grace of God, his opportunity lies shortly ahead.

Thoughts for Modern Jobs:

1. Make a list of grace notes you've seen in the story of Job.

2. Do you think Job has assurance of an afterlife, or does he expect everything to work out in his lifetime? Try to think from Job's point of view rather than as a person familiar with the New Testament.

3. How important is the afterlife to you in resolution of injustices that have been dealt to you here on earth?

Thoughts for Job's Caregivers:

1. How do you feel when you hear of a death-row inmate making a profession of faith?

2. Compare how you feel when you hear about the dying declaration of a saint.

3. How can you help your Job not only anticipate unmerited favor but live with unfavored merit?

11

NIGHT VISION

JOB 20:1—21:34

Upon this conviction [Job] rebuilds his faith, a faith based
upon vision rather than upon sight.

MARY ELLEN CHASE, IN PREFACE TO
THE BOOK OF JOB WITH PICTURES BY ARTHUR SZYK

————————

In my first novel, I took the name of one of Job's blowhard
visitors and gave it to the character [Zophar]
who is a pompous political columnist.

WILLIAM SAFIRE, *THE FIRST DISSIDENT:
THE BOOK OF JOB IN TODAY'S POLITICS*

————————

Nighttime was as sensitive a time of day for Job as it is for
most people who endure physical or emotional suffering. "When
I lie down," Job reported, "I say, 'When shall I rise? But the night
is long, and I am full of tossing until dawn'" (7:4). Zophar tests
Job's sleep-deprived patience with an accusation that Job lacks
understanding of his sinful nature. Zophar takes umbrage at being rebuked by Job. Short of patience, Job asks Zophar to do him
one little favor: let him have his say and then, if Zophar wants to,
mock on. Inspired by his own sense of enlightenment, Zophar
compares Job to a dream that flies away, "no more to be found,
banished like a vision of the night" (20:8).

Job and all of his friends have believed in a theology of prosperity, but now he—and he hopes his friends—must admit that there are plenty of examples of wicked men who enjoy prosperity. Job wants to see justice carried out in his lifetime rather than visited upon future generations to come. Let the wicked feel the full weight of God's wrath themselves! But Job is not the only one who lies awake at night.

If I asked you to choose a single word to describe your relationship with God when you go to bed at night, you might choose some of these words that friends of mine did when I asked them to use one word to describe their spiritual life. Many chose dark words like *shot, blank, zip, inconsistent, frustrating, under siege, running on empty, dry, flat-line.*

A friend of mine asked for an evening shift assignment as a hospital chaplain. Toby knew how shot, blank, zip, inconsistent, frustrating, under siege, running on empty, dry and flat-line the nights are for those who are in pain. Night terrors magnify suffering. In *The Gift of Pain,* Dr. Paul Brand tells the story of a war hero who disrupted a field hospital while he was "running on empty."[1]

An artillery shell had shattered Jake's legs while he was in battle. Despite these severe injuries, this soldier was able to crawl out of his foxhole and find a wounded friend who was still in the line of fire. Incredibly, the injured man was able to drag his buddy back to safety. Later in the evacuation hospital, when all the patients were awake and there was a lot of activity going on, Jake could handle the injections of the crude penicillin extract. The middle of the night injections, however, were beyond his ability to endure. As the night nurse approached his bed with the needle, this hero would cry like a baby and fight her off. Having heard of Jake's ability to endure great pain in battle, Dr. Brand asked him why a simple needle prick troubled him so much. "There's a lot more going on out there [on the battlefield]," Jake said, "the noise, the flashes, my buddies around me. But here in the ward, I have only one thing to think about all night in bed: that needle. It's huge, and when the nurse comes down the row with her tray full of syringes, it gets bigger and bigger."[1]

For poor Job, the torment got bigger and bigger at night. The same thing happens to my patients. I had a teenage patient with terminal cancer who had difficulty falling asleep at night. One night I brought my guitar to the hospital hoping that song would accomplish what words could not. Knowing that Eric's family were of German heritage, I started out with old-fashioned *Volkslieder*. His dad was so tickled that he called Eric's granddad and held the phone to my guitar as we schmaltzed along together. The next day we made a discharge plan for hospice care at home. If Eric was going to die, he wanted to die at home.

When I arrived at their home for my first post-discharge house call, Eric's grandfather was there at the house. Yes, *Opa* had a Christian background. No, he was not in a happy relationship with God these days. Especially at night. *Why Eric?* he asked on his pillow in the dark. Tears filled his eyes and anger at God occupied his heart whenever he thought that his beloved *Enkelkind* would die.

I took my guitar from its case and ran through my German repertoire. *Opa* had known most of these folk songs since childhood and sang heartily along. From his eyes I could see that he was back home in Germany. Then I switched to a different form of song. *Jesu, höchster Name* . . . "Jesus, Name above all names, beautiful Savior, glorious Lord, Emmanuel, God is with us, blessed Redeemer, living Word." Tears formed in the eyes of the embittered old man. The song was new to *Opa*, but the words spoke directly to his heart. With callused hands he swept the tears away from his eyes. "That's the most beautiful song I have ever heard in my life," he said. That night he turned his heart toward God.

If I were Zophar, I would have asked for the night shift with Job. Rather than debating with the suffering man by day, I would have sung about the blessed name of the Lord. That is just how Job started his ordeal. "The LORD gave, and the LORD has taken away. Blessed be the name of the LORD" (1:21 NRSV). Blessing God's name is a safe starting and ending place for us as well.

Thoughts for Modern Jobs:

1. Make a list of things you possess that if you lost them you could say, "The Lord gave, the Lord can take away. Blessed be the name of the Lord."

2. Are your children and grandchildren on that list?

3. Reflect on times in the night that fear and anger replaced the confidence you felt during the daylight hours.

Thoughts for Job's Caregivers:

1. What is meant by "the patience of Job" (James 5:11)?

2. How does Job's discourse with Zophar either illustrate or refute that he is an exemplary patient person?

3. How can you minister to a Job who has difficulty sleeping?

12

CAN A MORTAL BE OF USE TO GOD?

JOB 22:1—25:6

Every mother has a favorite child.
The one I've loved the most is the one whom I have watched
struggle and—because the struggle was his—done nothing.

ERMA BOMBECK, *FAVORITE CHILD*

During my darkest hours . . . all the neat Sunday school
answers I had learned as a kid seemed terribly hollow.
There are no pat answers for many terrible
and contradictory things in this broken world.

BRENT FOSTER, IN *FINDING GOD AT HARVARD*

Eliphaz the Temanite asked Job, "Can a mortal be of use to God? Can even the wisest be of service to him?" (22:2 NRSV). Eliphaz reminds me of questions I had about God as a child.

In Sunday school I memorized the Westminster Catechism (mercifully, the "Shorter Version") with its series of questions and answers. I've never forgotten the first question (and answer) because they evoked in me a deep sense of mystery:

Question: What is the chief end of Man?
Answer: Man's chief end is to glorify God, and to enjoy him forever.

Only a child would have the temerity to imagine the corollary question that was on my mind: *If my chief end is to glorify God and enjoy him forever, what is the chief end of God?* I posed this question to the pastor, a ripe young Calvinist recently plucked from a seminary vine. He acknowledged that my question was an excellent one. He spoke about the nature of God, including mysterious attributes he called "incommunicable." There are some qualities of God, he said, that his creatures may attain. But then God has other attributes that are far beyond sharing with mere mortals.

In an era when poliomyelitis was an ever-present plague, even a small child like me understood what it meant to be "communicable." I concluded that there are some parts of God's nature that are downright contagious. Other parts of his nature, however, I couldn't catch even if I wanted to. But it seemed to me that the pastor had slithered away before I could ask the deeper question that came from my heart, not my head: *Does God enjoy me?*

I wonder if Job asked himself the same question.

On the surface, Eliphaz's questions seem most modest, befitting of a creature standing humbly before the Creator. Bildad picks up this argument a few chapters later when he compares mere mortals to maggots (25:6). Their theological theme is compatible with the psalmist's ("What are human beings that you are mindful of them, mortals that you care for them?" Psalm 8:4 NRSV), but their phrasing lacks the tender rhetorical assurance of an honored place for us in God's grand scheme of things.

Eliphaz speaks of Job's relationship with God:

Is it any pleasure to the Almighty if you are righteous, or is it gain to him if you make your ways blameless? (22:3 NRSV)

Is it for your piety that he reproves you, and enters into judgment
with you? (22:4 NRSV)

Is not God high in the heavens? (22:12 NRSV)

The deity Eliphaz speaks of is a remote and distant God of
prosperity. So high in the heavens is this deity that he is totally
"incommunicable." This God demands righteousness from his
creatures, but he doesn't seem to enjoy what he has gained
through his demand. Eliphaz proposes to Job the remedy of repentance:

Agree with God, and be at peace; in this way good will come to
you. (22:21 NRSV)

If you return to the Almighty, you will be restored. (22:23 NRSV)

If the Almighty is your gold and your precious silver, then you will
delight yourself in the Almighty, and lift up your face to God.
(22:25-26 NRSV)

Throughout the history of faith, few human beings have been
more useful to God than his servant Job. The irony of Eliphaz's
theology is that he fails to express God's reciprocity of delight:

The LORD will again *delight* in you and make you prosperous.
(Deuteronomy 30:9)

[I will] be *glad and rejoice* forever in what I will create, for I will
create Jerusalem to be a *delight* and its people a *joy*. I will *rejoice*
over Jerusalem and take *delight* in my people. (Isaiah 65:18-19)

Is not Ephraim my dear son, the child in whom I *delight*? (Jere-
miah 31:20)

Throughout Scripture God reveals the use that he has for
mere mortals. He even has use for those who are not as blameless as Job:

Adam and Eve were of use to God even after they disobeyed in the Garden of Eden.

Abraham was of use to God after he lied about Sarah being his sister.

Rahab was of use to God after a life of prostitution.

King David was of use to God after he committed adultery with Bathsheba and murdered her husband.

Even to religious unbelievers the story of Job has come to typify Everyperson, a little guy or gal at the mercy of forces far more powerful than they are. The likes of you and me continue to be of use to God even when we're suffering—perhaps especially when we suffer:

Joni Eareckson Tada has been of more use to God quadriplegic in a wheelchair than she ever was standing on two feet.

Watergate conspirator Chuck Colson has been of more use to God because he went to prison.

Harvard student Brent Foster has been of more use to God afflicted by cancer than if he had enjoyed perfect health.

Each of these modern saints moved past the introspective derailment of "Why me?" to the affirmative statement, "Since it is me, this is what I'm going to do about it." None of these saints was resigned to a situation. "Resignation says, 'What a waste.' Acceptance asks, 'In what redemptive way will you use this mess, Lord?'"[1] Saintly stories are all about messes.

If Joni had retained her mobility . . .

If Chuck had been converted but never gone to jail . . .

If Brent had started Harvard as a healthy student . . .

If Job had retained his wealth and popularity . . .

Without their "ifs," what use would any of these stories be to us as fellow pilgrims? And if they were of no use to us, what possible use could they be to God?

Brent Foster is as comparable to Job as anyone I know. His high school friends called him the most accomplished, polished and courageous student who had ever graduated from their school. He was elected president of most major organizations in his high school. When he began his studies at Harvard, the world seemed to be at his feet. But his lungs were already full of metastatic cancer.

Like Job, Brent became strong when he was his weakest. The best that Job could do was to hold fast to his faith in and relationship with God. Near the end of his life Brent Foster echoed Job's words:

> When all the distractions and illusions we create for ourselves are washed away, all can appear empty and futile.... However, I now know that what remains after such a washing is all I really ever had to begin with: my faith in God, and the hope that things are working according to his will.[2]

With all due respect to statements of faith like the Westminster Catechism and the creeds that Brent Foster and I may have learned in our youth, it is only when Job and Brent and you and I come to those desperate moments that threaten to destroy our faith that we can dare to ask, "Does God enjoy me? Does God have any use for me?" Even as Brent's body weakened and each breath became a struggle, he would have used his last gasp to shout loud enough for all of us to hear, "You'd better believe it!"

Thoughts for Modern Jobs:

1. What use do you think that God has for you? What evidence do you have for that opinion?

2. Nowhere in the *Book of Job* do we read that God loves Job or that Job loves God. Job and God use other words to express the intimacy of their relationship. As you read *Job* did you see any clues to love on the part of either God or Job?

3. What other words do you sense in the *Book of Job* besides *love* and *grace* that you use to express your relationship with God?

Thoughts for Job's Caregivers:

1. Make a list of people you have ministered to whose stories show that they have been of use to God.

2. Help your Jobs make a list of things they believe with their heads but have difficulty believing in their heart of hearts.

3. How can you assure your Jobs that God enjoys them?

13

JOB'S TEARS

JOB 26:1—31:40

The whole world is dressed in tears,
and I have joined the procession.

ANN WEEMS, *PSALMS OF LAMENT*

I felt so bad that I groaned an Old Testament lamentation
AAAAIEOOOOW! to which responded a great silent
black man sitting next to me on the blocky couch:
"Ain't it the truth though." After that I felt better.

WALKER PERCY, *LOVE IN THE RUINS*

The fictional hero of Walker Percy's *Love in the Ruins*[1] was once a respected psychiatrist. The day that Dr. Tom More groaned his lament "AAAAIEOOOOW," the tables had just turned on him. The doctor had become a psychiatric patient himself, given to fits of melancholia. His colleagues furtively sought to heal him with their words. Alas, like Job's friends, More's colleagues were worthless physicians. Yet a fellow patient, a man of color, reared in quite different circumstances than the well-heeled white Southern doctor, was the only one who spoke healing words. This humble fellow sufferer validated More's lament: "Ain't it the truth though." After that the doctor could finally say that he felt better.

One aim of Scripture is to introduce us to fellow sufferers who can validate our laments. Although Job knew *AAAAIEOOOOW,* the man was no whiner. Consider Job's record before his affliction. When he took his place in the square at the gate of the city where he met Eliphaz, Bildad and Zophar, he did more than talk. He ministered to those who suffered. Job was a social activist:

> I delivered the poor who cried and the orphan who had no help. (29:12 NRSV)

> I caused the widow's heart to sing for joy. (29:13 NRSV)

> I was eyes to the blind and feet to the lame. (29:15 NRSV)

> I was a father to the needy. (29:16 NRSV)

> I championed the cause of the stranger. (29:16 NRSV)

> I broke the fangs of the unrighteous and made them drop their prey from their teeth. (29:17 NRSV)

> Did I not weep for those whose day was hard? (30:25 NRSV)

The record shows that Job's consistently righteous deeds were deeply appreciated by his beneficiaries. From his own mouth we learn that people listened to him and kept silence for his counsel (29:21). Once Job had taken his place as a chief and was the one to comfort mourners. Now he sits in an ash heap mourning without comfort. Who will listen now? Who will be Job's eyes and ears? Who will father him and champion his cause? Where is the community who will deliver him when he cries? Who will cause his heart to sing for joy? Not Eliphaz, Bildad and Zophar. Through the sarcasm of their accusations, they hold him in their fangs.

A modern Job named John Mark Hicks refers to the patriarch as a faithful lamenter.[2] He confirms that Job's tears were legitimate, his complaints grounded in fact. And he warns us that Job's friends are as much to be damned for their destruction of community as for their pitiful theology. Bad theology begets broken community.

Hicks tells the sad story of a pastor who was infected with the AIDS virus through a blood transfusion, not through any risky behavioral choice he had ever made. After the pastor told his congregation about his affliction, they dismissed him.[3] Even religious leaders need community. Perhaps especially our leaders need this wider expression of God's presence in our midst.

"Blessed are those who mourn," said Jesus to those like Job, "for they shall find comfort" (Matthew 5:4). Through their faithful lament blessed mourners will find a new and better community. Through their tears blessed mourners will connect with others who have found God on their ash heaps. Oswald Chambers puts it this way: "If we really face the teachings of Jesus Christ in the Sermon on the Mount honestly and drastically, we shall know something of what Job was going through."[4] In fact, the Sermon on the Mount reads like a job description for those who, like Job's comforters, would minister to the afflicted. The Sermon reads like a series of promises to Job:

> Blessed is poor-in-spirit Job, for before his trial is over he will possess all the riches of heaven.
> Blessed is mournful Job, for God himself will be his Comforter.
> Blessed is meek Job, for his earthly possessions will be restored.
> Blessed is hungry-and-thirsty Job, for God himself will fill him with his righteousness.
> Blessed is merciful Job. Don't we all need mercy?
> Blessed is pure-of-heart Job, because he's going to get his fondest wish—to see God in his flesh.

Blessed is peaceable Job, because God will call him a son.

Blessed is persecuted Job, for he will possess the kingdom of heaven.

Blessed is Job when his so-called friends insult him, persecute him and falsely say all kinds of evil against him. Rejoice, Job, because you aren't the first godly person who's ever been through this battle. And you surely won't be the last! Welcome to the new community, Job and everyone like you. Rejoice and be exceedingly glad.

Job may be Everyperson, but adversity does not bless us all. Nor do we want such a blessing! Unless we can hope in God even if he were to slay us (13:15), there is no blessing in our tears. In a lovely motet based on the story of Job, seventeenth-century composer Giacomo Carissimi assigns these words of blessing to an angel who guards Job against the wiles of the Evil One: "Happy is he who is taken up by the Lord. The Lord woundeth and healeth; he offendeth and he cureth." Together Job and the Angel pronounce a hauntingly beautiful benediction: "And these words will be always on my lips: Blessed be the name of the Lord."[5]

Like Job we can be faithful lamenters. Like the blessed poor, mournful, meek, hungry, merciful, pure, peaceable and persecuted, through our lament we become salt and light to a broken world (Matthew 5:13-14). Through our tears like blessed Job we can bear witness to the power of God in the world (27:11). Blessed be the name of the Lord who takes us up!

Thoughts for Modern Jobs:
1. Is there something that you have lost that you long for?
2. Has the community of faith ever hurt you in your longing?

3. How do you think the community of faith can help you in your longing?

Thoughts for Job's Caregivers:

1. Where do you see Job exhibit courage before his losses, while the losses were happening and after the losses occurred?

2. What other virtues besides courage do you see in Job's life?

3. Does your Job exhibit those virtues or need some encouragement to seek after them?

14

A Generational Clash

Job 32:1—37:34

The problem with the destructive elements in friendship
is that we discover them so slowly that we may have
destroyed the possibility of being friends
before we recognize the difficulty.

PAULA RIPPLE, *CALLED TO BE FRIENDS*

People resemble their times more
than they resemble their parents.

AN OLD ADAGE QUOTED BY RON ZEMKE,
CLAIRE RAINES & BOB FILIPCZAK IN *GENERATIONS AT WORK*

As a medical student I discovered a phenomenon that I dubbed "All patients are deaf unless proven otherwise." Too often, doctors (especially young surgeons) shouted at elderly patients before determining whether or not they had a hearing impairment. Equally often I would hear a patient shout back, "Stop shouting at me, Sonny! I'm not deeeeeeef!" Elihu, Job's fourth visitor, speaks at this volume level.

Apparently, as he held his tongue, Elihu's anger has been building up. Now he tells Job that he waited to speak up because he was younger than the others. "I am young in years, and you are old," he says, "that is why I was fearful, not daring to tell you what I know" (32:6). When he finally opens his mouth, Elihu loses whatever courtesy he intended toward an elder.

Elihu spins from one speech to another, his wrath spilling over from Job onto the other three visitors. "I waited while you spoke," he says to Eliphaz, Bildad and Zophar. "I listened to your reasoning; while you were searching for words, I gave you my full attention. But not one of you has proved Job wrong; none of you has answered his arguments" (32:11-12).

So angry is Elihu that he reels off four serial monologues before Job has a chance to respond to any one of them. "Pay heed, Job," he warns the suffering man, "listen to me; be silent and I will speak" (33:31). In the first three cycles of three speeches each by Eliphaz, Bildad and Zophar, Job's responses were longer than the advice he had subsequently received. So offensive is Elihu's rhetoric in his four rapid-fire speeches that God doesn't give Job the opportunity to answer his critic.

In contrast to Job's other friends, Elihu was not a team player. It was he, not they, who brought age into the equation. In our own times we see similar problems erupt in the workplace, not only from chronological age differences but from cultural generations that separate those of diverse age groups. For example, corporations see tensions when technogeeky Gen-Xers and Nexters team with technophobic boomers and builders. Rather than seeing mixed generational teams as a blend of differing skills and perspectives, most of us prefer to cluster with those who share our opinions and values. As Elihu did, we may harshly judge someone whose experience differs from our own. It is easier to empathize with someone whose experience is just like ours.

One of my young adult patients who was a ten-year survivor of advanced-stage Hodgkin's disease asked for my advice about his father. A recent college graduate, Norm was adept with the Internet. When his dad received a diagnosis of cancer, Norm quickly amassed a large body of information on his father's disease. Not only did he find a data base with all the clinical trials in the country about that form of cancer, but he came up with the names and phone numbers of the top doctors in the field. From his conversation with his father, Norm had heard that the prognosis was serious and his father might not be cured from this cancer. Proud that his own skills had supplemented his loving motivation, Norm drove home for the weekend (his father did not use e-mail) with his cache of data about a possible cure.

"Thanks, son," his father told him, "but I like my doctors. I'll go with what they advise."

Norm was so upset with his father's behavior that he stopped by my office to enlist my support. "He's not thinking clearly," Norm opined. "You're more his own age group. Maybe he'll listen to you."

Actually, I had already spoken with Norm's dad. He had stopped by my office the day he got his diagnosis. "I hear what the doctors are saying, and I realize that it isn't particularly encouraging. But I know they're good doctors, and honest. The tricky part will be dealing with Norman. He was very upset when I called and told him. He wanted to fly straight home as if I was dying. The hard part will be making him realize that this is my cancer, not his."

Just as Norm's dad gave him credit for his intelligence and

caring, I want to give young Elihu credit for his motivation. He was passionately committed to the person and the principle, even if it was principle as he saw it. We need people in this world who keep their eyes firmly fixed on important issues. Job was such a man, risking intimacy with his wife to maintain personal integrity. But we also see the risks of issue orientation from the dialogues in the text. Taken to its worst extreme, a passion for principles can lead to nasty confrontation.

In his four speeches, Elihu outlines what he sees as the issues at hand:

1. God allows suffering to turn a soul back from the Pit (33:29-30).

2. God repays us for what we have done and brings upon us what our conduct deserves (34:11).

3. God does not listen to empty pleas (35:13).

4. God's ways are beyond our understanding (36:26; 37:5, 23).

My patient Norm was upset that I was not willing to join him in his war on his father's cancer. He had hoped that my age and maturity would lend credulity to his argument. Elihu's complaint with the other visitors was not with their theology but with their inability to persuade Job that these mishaps were a warning from God about sin in his life. None of these characters in *Job*, least of all Elihu, had the opposite problem that sometimes befalls folks who prize relationships above issues—conflict avoidance.

Job is a book about principles and people who prize principles. But from the moment when Satan strolls up to heaven, we notice the importance of issues to the human relationships in the story. We empathize with Job. We expect God to treat a blameless man far better. You and I, not Job and not his friends, are the ones who would like to avoid the conflicts that must surely follow.

As we interact with the *Book of Job*, we cannot escape the fact that both principles and relationships are important. There is a kernel of truth in each of the issues that Elihu outlines. The problem is that they don't apply to Job's situation. Principles matter, but it also matters a great deal to us how friends and acquaintances deal with suffering people.

Mercifully, God interrupts Elihu before Job is obliged to respond. No, Elihu, the Almighty is not beyond reach. You are about to find out just how accessible he is.

Thoughts for Modern Jobs:

1. Why was Elihu angry at Job? At the other three friends?

2. What could Elihu learn about speaking the truth in love?

3. By nature are you more likely to take an issue to extremes (confrontation) or give more importance to relationships than they are entitled to (conflict avoidance)?

Thoughts for Job's Caregivers:

1. How do age and family rank play out in your Job's story?

2. In your Job's family, which members are issue-oriented and which are relational?

3. How can you help your Job's family to work together as a team?

SECTION IV

~⟡~

COSMIC QUESTIONS

[Job's] question, the harrowing
question of someone who has only
heard of God, is "Why me?"
There is no answer,
because it is the wrong question.

STEPHEN MILLER, *THE BOOK OF JOB*

15

DO YOU KNOW WHEN THE MOUNTAIN GOATS GIVE BIRTH?

JOB 38:1—39:30

If we should forget Darwin's theory for this evening
and believe that Adam was the first man,
we find that Adam is the first Faust, Job the second.

ARRIGO BOITO, IN NOTES FOR HIS OPERA *MEFISTOPHELE*

I think back to God's questions to Job:
"Have you ever given orders to the morning?
Do you hunt the prey for the lioness?"
And like a young apprentice in the presence of a master,
something in my heart says cautiously (yet eagerly),
"No, but I'd like to!"

JOHN ELDREDGE, *THE JOURNEY OF DESIRE*

Some of us have deep doubts about theories of science, and others may have serious questions about matters of faith. Many of us have moments when we wonder about both. To resolve those uncertainties we typically take the path of reason—Adam's munch on the forbidden fruit, Faust's focus on his learned books, or even

Job's analytical questions. By asking "Why me?" we apply what we think we know about God to our current predicaments.

Throughout the story Job has longed to be able to pose his question directly to God. Finally, in four long chapters (38:1—41:34), God appears to Job. *Revelation!* Rather than using the language of the justice system with which Job and his friends have framed their arguments, God prefers to chat about creation. Not once does God address the *why* question that has tormented Job. But Job's mood changes dramatically as he listens to his Maker describe his making. Better to be compared to a mountain goat than to be cosmically ignored!

A teenage patient once challenged me as a scientist and a person of faith.[1] In the days before his death, Scotty had cosmic questions in mind. "You know," he told me, "not everything in science is true. And not everything in religion either."

From where I was sitting it appeared that science had just failed this young man in a very big way. Scotty had vigorously pursued a cure for his cancer, but it had come back with a vengeance. "What is it in science that you have difficulty believing?" I asked him.

"They say that the world came about by accident," Scotty told me, "but when I look at the world and everything in it, I see a design and a plan. I could be wrong, but I doubt it." Scotty folded his arms across his chest, firming up his position. Amazing, I thought, that this young Job cares who is in attendance when mountain goats give birth.

With science put squarely in its place, we moved on to his other areas of doubt. "What is it about religion that you have trouble believing?" I asked him.

"Well, take David and Goliath, for instance." *David and Goliath? Why would a child have difficulty with the story of David and Goliath?* I wondered. My mind wandered back to countless Sunday school classrooms where wide-eyed, giggling little ones grinned their approval as the slingshot made its mark on the evil giant's forehead. "What is your problem with David and Goliath?" I asked him.

"Well, they say that Goliath was eight feet four, and there is nobody that tall," Scotty said firmly.

I couldn't leave the argument alone! His challenge was important, but it was also fun. "I've seen some pretty tall basketball players in my time," I countered.

"Not that tall," he insisted.

I was losing the argument so I got medical. "There's this pituitary condition where you keep making more and more growth hormone, and you keep growing and growing and growing."

"Not that tall," Scotty said. His arms recrossed his chest to hold his position tight, but then he became very quiet. "You know," he said softly, "it's not the details that matter. It's the moral of the story."

I was speechless, and so was Scotty's mother who had been standing by the bedside wondering all this time, *Is this* my *son talking?* I thought about this boy immersed in the terrifying world of high-tech medicine. And then I thought about David and Goliath. Just what was the moral of these stories, young Scotty's and young David's?

Both stories are tales of little lads who would prevail against something that was *unbelievably big*. As unbelievably big as a mean giant. As unbelievably big as cruel death.

In two astonishing minutes Scotty placed the cosmos in perspective. In four stunning poetic chapters God moves out of a storm and uses creation to answer Job's unanswerable questions. After all, it was Job who first appealed to nature. "Ask the animals and they will teach you" (12:7), he said to Zophar. Like us,

Job would prefer analogies to small weak animals like the ravens Jesus said his Father would care for (Luke 12:24). But large animals and wild ones? God shifts the focus of the argument from things humans can control to things outside our domination.

Some would say that today science can answer many of Job's and Scotty's questions. Science, however, lacks the passionate love expressed by the divine interrogatory Poet who takes center stage in these chapters.

Where . . .

were you when I laid the earth's foundation? (38:4)

does the darkness reside? (38:19)

What . . .

is the way to the abode of light? (38:19)

is the way to the place where lightning is dispersed? (38:24)

is the way to the place where the east winds are scattered over the earth? (38:24)

Who . . .

marked off the earth's dimensions? (38:5)

stretched a measuring line across the earth? (38:5)

laid earth's cornerstone? (38:6)

shut up the sea behind doors? (38:8)

made the clouds its garment? (38:9)

wrapped the sea in thick darkness? (38:9)

fixed limits for the sea? (38:10)

set the sea's doors and bars in place? (38:10)

said the sea may come this far and no farther? (38:11)

cuts a channel for the torrents of rain? (38:25)

cuts a path for the thunderstorm? (38:25)

fathers the drops of dew? (38:28)

gives birth to the frost? (38:29)

endowed the heart with wisdom? (38:36)

gave understanding to the mind? (38:36)

has the wisdom to count the clouds? (38:37)

can tip over the water jars of the heavens? (38:37)

provides food for the raven? (38:41)

let the wild donkey go free? (39:5)

untied the wild donkey's ropes? (39:5)

By way of contrast, God asks mere mortals:
Have you . . .

ever given orders to the morning? (38:12)

shown the dawn its place? (38:12)

journeyed to the springs of the sea? (38:16)

walked in the recesses of the deep? (38:16)

ever been shown the gates of death? (38:17)

comprehended the vast expanses of the earth? (38:18)

entered the storehouses of the snow? (38:22)

seen the storehouses of the hail? (38:22)

Can you . . .

take [light and darkness] to their places? (38:20)

bind the beautiful Pleiades? (38:31)

loose the cords of Orion? (38:31)

bring forth the constellations in their seasons? (38:32)

lead out the Bear with its cubs? (38:32)

set up God's dominion over the earth? (38:33)

raise your voice to the clouds? (38:34)

cover yourself with a flood of water? (38:34)

hold the wild ox to the furrow with a harness? (39:10)

trust a wild ox to bring in your grain? (39:12)

Do you . . .

know the laws of the heavens? (38:33)

hunt the prey for the lioness? (38:39)

satisfy the hunger of the lions? (38:39)

know when the mountain goats give birth? (39:1)

watch when the doe bears her fawn? (39:1)

count the months till the mountain goats and fawns bear? (39:2)

know the time they give birth? (39:2)

give the horse its strength? (39:19)

make the horse leap like a locust? (39:19)

⟨⟩

As young as Scotty was, he knew who made horses leap like locusts and who attended the birth of every baby mountain goat. Moreover he was confident that this same Person would be there with him to the end of his days. In *Job's* tender couplets, God is the one who asks the questions. Never once does God ask or answer *why*? The moral to Job's story and to Scotty's is *Who*.

Thoughts for Modern Jobs:

1. Have you ever been passionate about the work of your hands? Did anyone else share your level of enthusiasm for your creation?

2. Have you ever had a humbling experience that was so exhilarating that it lifted you up to a loftier place than you had ever reached before?

3. Have you ever had the feeling that God was saying to you, "Excuse me! Can we get things in perspective here?" What was the outcome of that experience?

Thoughts for Job's Caregivers:

1. How can you use the creation story in Genesis to bring your Job's story into perspective?

2. How can you use nature to help your Job see a design and a plan for his or her life?

3. How can you help your Job find the moral to his or her story?

16

~~~~~

CAN YOU PULL IN
THE LEVIATHAN
WITH A FISHHOOK?

JOB 40:1—41:34

We reach the rhapsody on Leviathan,
a fit crescendo that overwhelms Job at the last.

FRANCIS I. ANDERSON, *JOB: AN INTRODUCTION AND COMMENTARY*

Oh look—the deep, wide sea, brimming with fish past
counting, sardines and sharks and salmon.
Ships plow those waters and Leviathan,
your pet dragon, romps in them.

PSALM 104:24-26 THE MESSAGE

There are some things in nature that are just plain logical.
As a songwriter once noted, fish gotta swim and birds gotta fly.
Nature will act naturally. Even so, as large as leviathan is, as big
as behemoth may be, as huge as hippo hopes to grow, there are
cosmic questions that are naturally larger than they—and we—
are. When we wrestle with those questions, we hear God con-
necting questions of his own:

Do you . . .

have an arm like God's? (40:9)

Can you . . .

pull in the leviathan with a fishhook? (41:1)

tie the leviathan's tongue with a rope? (41:1)

put a cord through a leviathan's nose? (41:2)

pierce a leviathan's jaw with a hook? (41:2)

make a pet of the leviathan like a bird? (41:5)

put the leviathan on a leash for your girls? (41:5)

fill the leviathan's hide with harpoons? (41:7)

Would you . . .

discredit God's justice? (40:8)

condemn God to justify yourself? (40:8)

Who . . .

has a claim against God? (41:11)

obscures God's counsel without knowledge? (42:3)

can strip off the leviathan's outer coat? (41:13)

dares open the doors of the leviathan's mouth ringed about with fearsome teeth? (41:14)

After the Creator's first grand monologue about nature, Job falls silent. He places his hand over his mouth. Like the powerful sea creature leviathan, God illustrates that mortals cannot catch and tame him for our own purposes. As the subject turns to justice, God tells Job to brace himself for more questions.

In *Out of the Saltshaker* Rebecca Pippert tells about her experience as a student in a college biology class. On the first day of class her professor said that humans are "merely a fortuitous concourse of atoms, a meaningless piece of protoplasm in an absurd world."[1] Later that semester he shared his anguish in class about his daughter who had run away to live with an older man. "She will be deeply wounded," the professor mourned. "She will scar, and I can't do anything to help."

Pippert raised her hand and quietly asked how, according to his system of thinking, mere protoplasm could scar.

"Touché," he responded. "I could never regard my daughter as a set of chemicals, never. I can't take my beliefs that far."

Job needed beliefs that could carry him that far and further. God, we learn through his interrogation of Job, is so much greater than we are that we cannot make him into our domesticated pet. Neither can we cut him down to size and sell him off in docile doses or minuscule molecules.

Like Job I grew up to be a person of faith. Although God would hardly have chosen me to represent him in a contest with Satan, my intention as a young person was to live a godly life. But something happened during medical school when I was introduced to innocent suffering. God wasn't behaving the way I imagined a good God should act. Didn't the children I saw dying of cancer deserve a moral deity who played by rules of justice?

When I couldn't tame God or cut him down to size, I turned my back on faith and the book of faith. My only contact with the Bible came when I sang with an oratorio society. One great sacred piece I remember especially was Johannes Brahms's *ein deutsches Requiem*, written by a composer who described himself as an agnostic for much of his life. The mood of the second movement fits Job's state of depression and draws in part from Job's themes. Although the composer struggled with personal belief, he could not state the problem without reaching for a Scripture-promised resolution:

> Then all flesh is as grass, and all human glory is as the flower of grass. The grass withers and the flower falls away. . . . But the word of the Lord endures eternally. The redeemed of the Lord

will return and come to Zion with songs and everlasting joy upon their heads. (Isaiah 40:6-8; Job 14:2; Isaiah 51:11)[2]

Job himself hoped for redemption (19:25). Although his flesh was as fragile as grass, his heart yearned within him to see God with his own eyes (19:26-27). If Job had hope, that also came from God. If he had an argument, that also came from the Author of all valid questions.

For many years I continued to argue. My imagination was too limited to form a God big enough to pull in a leviathan with a fishhook, or big enough to deal with the problem of innocent suffering. Then I did what Job's friends should have done. I sat silently at the bedside of a child who was dying. I offered no platitudes of science or faith. I simply listened. God didn't need another angel that day because he sent an entire heavenly host for little Anna. In the moment of her death, the child testified to what she saw and heard. Angels came to accompany her to heaven with songs more beautiful than any music she had ever heard here on earth. I cannot think of Anna without hearing the angel prologue from *Mefistophele*. Anna set aside her own imagination that, like mine, might have been a tad too small for the occasion. She saw for herself with her own eyes. *Revelation*. The God who created the vast universe cared about a little child. *Ave, Signor degli angeli e dei santi!*

"Would you discredit God's justice?" God asked Job, then many years later asked me. Perhaps my "god" who didn't exist or didn't care was a deity far too small. I had just seen a child entering Zion with singing and everlasting joy. And in the story we're reading here, Job's redemption draws nigh as well.

Thoughts for Modern Jobs:
1. Read back through Job's responses to his friends. In what

ways does Job try to cut God down to a manageable size?

2. Can you think of a situation in which you tried to reduce God to a size that you could better understand? What was the outcome?

3. Describe a situation where you felt you had been treated unjustly and expected God to take your side. What was the outcome?

Thoughts for Job's Caregivers:

1. How can you help your Job understand that although God is too great to be cut down to size, he is still approachable?

2. What injustices does your Job see in his or her suffering?

3. What hope does your Job find in the words "I know that my Redeemer lives"? What does your Job hoped to be redeemed from?

17

THINGS TOO WONDERFUL FOR JOB TO HAVE KNOWN

JOB 42:1-6

So it was that to Job, when once the veil of flesh had been rent
by affliction, the world's stark beauty was revealed.

SIMONE WEIL, *PENSÉE SANS ORDRE*

It's like finger painting with Picasso,
but as God takes my hand the paint on his melds with mine.
A new color is born.

SHIELA WALSH, *HONESTLY*

Job admits that before his affliction his entire experience of God had been by hearsay. Yes, he had been a faithful believer. After all, God had chosen him for this test because of his blamelessness. But God's eloquent rhapsodies on creation come as a humbling surprise to the suffering man. Oswald Chambers said it this way:

Everything a man takes to be the key to a problem is apt to turn out another lock. . . . The creed Job held, which pretended to be a

key to the character of God, turned out to be a lock, and Job is re-
alizing that the only key to life is not a statement of faith in God,
nor an intellectual conception of God, but a personal relationship to him.[1]

If God had not stopped the theologians' mouths and chosen
to speak for himself, what conclusions might Job have reached
about the most miserable experience of his life? Rather than
words, Job needed evidence of God.

My dear friend Elke fell sick on a trip to Egypt one year. At
first she thought that the fevers and sweats were from malaria,
but an x-ray at a local hospital hinted at a far worse diagnosis.
Soon she was on a plane home to Germany to learn that she had
the most advanced stage possible of Hodgkin's disease. No wonder she had lost so much weight in recent months! Her husband
faxed me her oncologist's recommendation—intensive chemotherapy. The protocol was similar to the regimen that I used for
my Hodgkin's patients. Tough but effective. I knew from experience that it is so tough that more than a few adults stop their
treatment halfway through. The children I treat have parents to
encourage or bully them through. I wanted to make sure that
Elke wouldn't lose heart.

I made a packet of patient education brochures and brought
them with me to Germany. As Elke thumbed through them, she
found tips and facts that her doctors had never given her. I felt
relieved that there was something I could do to help. But it was
not my information that carried Elke through the long months
and multiple cycles of intensive chemotherapy. Instead, she took
her encouragement from a recurring symbol of a living, loving,
caring God.

Before each round of chemotherapy, Elke went to the hospital to have her blood counts checked. If her white blood cells were high enough, she would stay for the chemo. If not, she went home and waited for another day. For a busy person, it was a hard way to plan a life. But Elke knew by the morning exactly which days her blood counts would be high enough for treatment.

The bouquets came a variety of ways. Sometimes a friend stopped by to deliver one personally. Other times they came by way of a teleflorist. None of these friends had consulted with each other or made a plan. But Elke knew that if there was a gift of flowers that day, her blood counts would be high enough to get her chemo. She saw the flowers as a gift from God, a sign to help her through.

There were days when Elke couldn't walk a single block. There were nights when her husband held her head while she vomited. But if the flowers came, she knew that the God of the universe was with her to carry her through. He cared not only when mountain goats might give birth (39:12) but also when a sick young woman was ready for chemotherapy.

God appeared, and Job regained his courage. If Job had been God, he would have designed his life without the skin disease and all his losses. If it had been up to Elke, she never would have chosen Hodgkin's disease or its treatment. We are truly the most blessed of creatures when something happens in our lives that allows us to join with Job and Elke to tell God, "My ears had heard of you, but now my eyes have seen."

Elke completed treatment eleven years ago and has never relapsed. Today she still smiles with special delight when you bring her the gift of flowers.

Thoughts for Modern Jobs:

1. Have you ever had an experience in which God in some way revealed himself to you through his creation? What was your reaction to that experience?

2. What did you learn about God through his cosmic questions that you never before knew?

3. If you were the defense attorney defending Job's friends before the Judge, would you recommend a plea bargain to your clients or argue that they are not guilty of the charges?

Thoughts for Job's Caregivers:

1. Have your Job make a list of things "too wonderful to have known" before this current illness or crisis.

2. How can you help your Job open eyes and not just ears?

3. How can you put your Job in touch with God's revelation?

Epilogue

~~~

A SONG
OF RESTORATION

JOB 42:10-17

These gifts at the end are gestures of grace,
not rewards of virtue.

FRANCIS I. ANDERSON, *JOB: AN INTRODUCTION AND COMMENTARY*

God takes our training so seriously
because he fully intends to promote us.

JOHN ELDREDGE, *THE JOURNEY OF DESIRE*

Inevitably this book must come to a final chapter, but with that conclusion I know that Job and I are not finished with each other yet. To paraphrase Plato, in whatever direction I go, I will meet Job on the way back. For me there will always be another Job. For every Papa who hugs him today in heaven, there will be an Everyperson from Anytown whose journey to Uz has only just begun.

The conclusion of the *Book of Job* has long been a source of controversy. To some scholars, its happy-ever-after tone suggests that it was tagged on by later scribes rather than being an authentic part of Job's story. But for between-the-wars Austrian-Jewish writer Joseph Roth, the *Book of Job* ends with a messianic song.[1]

Mendel Singer, a simple man who teaches the Torah to little boys, leaves tsarist Russia for the garment district of New York City. The Singer family leaves one child behind, Menuchim, an epileptic who has never said any word other than *mamma*. The esteemed rabbi of Kluczÿsk had prophesied that Menuchim would be healed. "Do not leave him, stay with him, as though he were a healthy child," the Rabbi told his mother. But the family does leave him and the Bolshevik Revolution prevents them from bringing him to join them later.

One day a package arrives, and in it is a record of "Menuchim's Song." Everyone who hears the song acknowledges that they have never in their lives heard such beautiful music. On the first night of Passover, Mendel and friends set a place for Elijah as they have every Seder Eve of their lives. Unexpectedly there is a knock on the door. They who had waited for the Messiah's forerunner all their lives think that it must be the wind. But a stranger enters and they invite him to sit at table with them.

"Do not let me interrupt you," says the stranger. "Please go on with your prayers."[2] Despite his bitterness at all the losses in his life, Mendel joins in the "Hallelujah!" at the end of each strophe. He shakes his head so vigorously that his long beard seems to take part in the prayers which his mouth has reluctantly celebrated of late. As the humble folk at table pronounce the final blessing—next year in Jerusalem!—Mendel turns to their visitor and asks what he has come to tell them.

Their visitor is the composer of "Menuchim's Song," Menuchim himself, healed by a worthwhile physician who took him into his own home as the rabbi had prophesied. Mendel, who for many years had cradled the mute boy in his arms, sits like a child himself on his son Menuchim's knees and repeats the words of the prophecy. "Pain will make him wise, ugliness good, bitterness mild, and sickness strong."[3] Mendel falls asleep and rests "from the burden of his happiness, and the greatness of the miracle."[4]

The *Book of Job* is a song about a great miracle, that the God of the universe who holds all the answers to life's questions knows and loves us. Even in our trials, God puts his song of great hope on our lips. Job is Everyperson with as many variations possible for restoration as there are and will be Jobs on this earth. Recently I met him in a way that I have never known him before. As long as this earth endures, there will always be a new stanza to the song.

I hadn't seen Markus, a German pastor, for several years. Mutual friends had alerted me that something distressing had happened in his life. Two months before my visit, Markus had signed a release for his medical records in applying for some life insurance. The insurance company informed him that because he had multiple sclerosis, he wasn't eligible for coverage. *Multiple sclerosis?* Although his records contained the diagnosis, his doctors had never told him that they suspected this dread disease. It was a shock to hear this type of news in such a careless manner. His trust in the "worthless physicians" who had withheld the information from him was fatally shattered. Not only must he face an uncertain future, but he must find new doctors.

We sat at the kitchen table and shared a typical German *Abendbrot*. Jonas and Leonard, his two young sons, told me all about their trip to California. When we were finished, Antje shooed them to their bedroom to get on their pajamas. I smiled watching Markus kiss Jonas and Leonard good night. One of the things I've always appreciated about him is his love for his children. It's a pleasure to be a guest in the home of a man who considers fatherhood a high and holy calling.

When his paternal chores were complete, Markus settled comfortably on his living room sofa across from me so we could chat. Until that moment, neither one of us had mentioned his illness, but he guessed correctly that our friends would have told me. "I'm not a sick man," Markus started, "I'm a healthy man with a diagnosis."

He was neither hunched up nor stooped over as he spoke. His arms spread along the top of the sofa, a view of his beloved Marburg framed in the window behind him. Markus was an open and happy man. The last phrase I would have used to describe him was "in denial."

For several years Markus had noted numbness in his left arm and leg. That's why he had gone to his family doctor in the first place, and later to see a neurologist. When he confronted his physicians with the information they had withheld from him, they claimed that he hadn't fit all the diagnostic criteria of MS at the time they had seen him. They hadn't wanted him to worry!

Markus found new doctors and went through a further series of tests. There was no question that he fit the diagnostic criteria for MS. Courageously he surrendered his privacy and told his friends what he knew so that they would hear accurate facts directly from him. But he has no motor weakness as of yet. In fact, at forty years of age he is jogging, swimming and riding his bicycle more than he ever has before. Markus draws encouragement from his physical endurance. Perhaps he will be one of the minority of MS patients whose condition declines no further. I hope so.

Instead of following through with the position he had sought in congregational ministry, Markus started a new career as a hospital chaplain. His first patient was a pastor from his own denomination who was only four years his senior. The man was dying in an intensive care unit on life support machines. That was hard on the "man with a diagnosis." His hospital turf also covered pediatrics, oncology and even the neurology ward where he would doubtless see patients with various stages of MS.

After a few rough weeks Markus found that he loved this work. He felt at home with the sick and looked forward to serving them. Then at a youth conference, he ran into a teenager he had met several years before.

"Markus!" the young man greeted him, "I heard about your dreadful diagnosis!" Unlike the last time they had spoken, the teen was not standing with him shoulder to shoulder. He was sitting in a wheelchair. In a swimming accident, he had dived into shallow water and damaged his spinal cord irreparably. Since then he could not move from mid-chest down.

"What about you?" Markus asked. "I'm still a healthy man. You, on the other hand, are sitting in a wheelchair. Isn't your situation worse than mine?"

"Oh, no!" the young man blurted out. "My future is certain; yours is not. The worst that could happen to me has already come to pass. You, on the other hand, don't know what the future holds."

Markus was both startled and strangely encouraged by this awkward encounter. Each of them thought that he was better off than the other! He wondered, *Is that what God meant when he said that through the sufficiency of his grace he will never give us more than we can bear?*

Oh yes, Markus has met his share of "empathic failures" since learning his diagnosis. But by the grace of God he is still standing tall. "Man is born broken," said Eugene O'Neill. "He lives by mending. The grace of God is glue."[5] Clearly Markus is a well-glued-together man.

Although we know that Job's friends visited for at least seven days, the scribe of Scripture doesn't tell us how long his entire ordeal lasted. The forty-two chapters of the *Book of Job* seem to take forever. In comparison, Markus's two-month journey through "Why me?" seemed mercifully brief. As we continued our conversation, he turned from "Why?" to "Who?"

"You know," Markus reflected, "if God were to take me today, that would be all right. I've had a wonderful life, and I'm only grateful. But if I could live, I have three wishes. First, I'd like to see my sons grown up. Second, if possible, I'd like to see my grandchildren. And third, I'd like to see my Antje when she's sixty."

His voice cracked a bit as he finished sharing his third wish. Markus had a moist sparkle in his eyes as if he was expecting to like what he saw of his wife at that age. And my eyes started to fill as well. I have never heard a man place as beautiful a blessing on his wife.

Before I left I asked Markus, "When I'm praying for you, what would you like me to pray for?" My question caught my friend by surprise.

Some years ago another pastor had told me a story from his experience as a hospital chaplain. In the neurological ICU he called on a young man left quadriplegic by a motorcycle accident. He asked him the same question I had just asked Markus: "What would you like prayer for?" The chaplain wondered what he would hear. Probably the man would ask for strength to endure what was yet to come. But his patient didn't ask for strength. Instead he said, "I want to walk again!"

Now Markus thought long about my question while I imagined what he would request. Then, with clarity he replied, "Pray for the patients I minister to at the hospital. That's the prayer I would like."

After Job had prayed for his friends, the Lord made him prosperous again and gave him twice as much as he had before.... After this, Job lived a hundred and forty years; he saw his children and their children to the fourth generation. And so he died, old and full of years. (42:10, 16-17)

Thoughts for Modern Jobs:

1. Can you recall a time when you snapped out of depression by focusing on the needs of somebody else rather than feeling sorry for yourself?

2. What unanswered question(s) do you still have for God about Job's story?

3. If I asked you what you would like prayer for, what would your request be?

Thoughts for Job's Caregivers:

1. What different forms of restoration are possible for your Job?

2. How do you help a Job live with uncertainty?

3. If I asked you what you would like prayer for, what would your request be? (If you'd like, both "Modern Jobs" and "Job's Caregivers" are welcome to email their requests to me at <DoktorDi@aol.com>.)

Notes

Preface
[1]Diane Komp, *Hope Springs from Mended Places: Images of Grace in the Shadows of Life* (Grand Rapids, Mich.: Zondervan, 1994).
[2]William Safire, *The First Dissident: The Book of Job in Today's Politics* (New York: Random House, 1992), p. xix.

Prologue
[1]Gustavo Gutiérrez, *Job: God-Talk and the Suffering of the Innocent* (Maryknoll, N.Y.: Orbis, 1987).

Chapter 1: Enter the Accuser
[1]*Mefistophele* or *Mephistophele* means "he who does not love light."
[2]Arrigo Boito, *Mefistophele*, trans. Avril Bardoni, copyright 1984 DECCA Records.

Chapter 3: The Case of the Wannabe Widow
[1]Samuel Terrien, *The Iconography of Job Through the Centuries: Artists as Biblical Interpreters* (University Park: Pennsylvania State University Press, 1996), p. 141.
[2]<http://sgwwwepfl.ch/BERGER/LaTour/job.htm>.
[3]Andrew Wright, *Blake's Job: A Commentary* (Oxford: Oxford University Press, 1972), p. 20.
[4]Neil Simon, *God's Favorite* (New York: Samuel French, 1975).
[5]Robert Frost, *The Masque of Reason* (New York: Henry Holt, 1945).
[6]Muriel Spark, *The Only Problem* (Franklin Center, Penn.: Franklin Library, 1984).
7Archibald MacLeish, *J. B.* (New York: Samuel French, 1958)
[8]Diane M. Komp: *Anatomy of a Lie: The Truth About Lies and Why Good People Tell Them* (Grand Rapids, Mich.: Zondervan, 1998).
[9]Steven A. Carter, *Integrity* (New York: BasicBooks, 1996), p. 7.

Chapter 4: Empathic Failures
[1]Shiva is a Jewish mourning ritual. Friends and relative visit the family home for seven days following a death. In Hebrew the word *Shevah* means "seven."
[2]In Howard Spiro et al., eds., *Empathy and the Practice of Medicine* (New Haven, Conn.: Yale University Press, 1993), p. 8, sympathy is expressed as the statement

"I want to help you" while empathy says "I could *be* you."

Chapter 5: Job Wishes He Had Never Been Born
[1]This passage is a mildly modernized version of Jeremy Taylor's poetic setting that was set to music by Henry Purcell as "Job's Curse," Z191 (1688).

Chapter 7: The Problem of Argument
[1]Muriel Spark, *The Only Problem* (Franklin Center, Penn.: Franklin Library, 1987), p. 22.

Chapter 8: Worthless Physicians
[1]Larry Dossey, *Healing Words: The Power of Prayer and the Practice of Medicine* (San Francisco: HarperCollins, 1993), p. xvii.
[2]John Mark Hicks, *Yet Will I Trust Him: Understanding God in a Suffering World* (Joplin, Mo.: College Press, 1999), p. 42.

Chapter 9: Empty Notions
[1]Harold S. Kushner, *When Bad Things Happen to Good People* (New York: Schocken, 1981).
[2]Progeria is a lethal syndrome characterized by premature aging.
[3]Moses Maimonides, *The Guide for the Perplexed* (New York: Dover, 1956), p. 302.

Chapter 10: Unfavored Merit
[1]Neil Simon, *God's Favorite* (New York: Random House, 1975).
[2]Karl Barth, *Dogmatics in Outline* (New York: Harper & Row, 1959), p. 15.

Chapter 11: Night Vision
[1]Paul Brand and Philip Yancey, *The Gift of Pain* (New York: HarperCollins, 1993), pp. 39-40.

Chapter 12: Can A Mortal Be of Use to God?
[1]Elisabeth Elliot, "Lord if I Ever Needed You, It's Now!" quoted in Creath Davis, *Portraits of Perseverance* (Grand Rapids, Mich.: Baker, 1987), p. 32.
[2]Kelly Monroe, *Finding God at Harvard* (Grand Rapids, Mich.: Zondervan, 1996), p. 132.

Chapter 13: Job's Tears
[1]Walker Percy, *Love in the Ruins* (New York: Ballantine, 1971), p. 90.
[2]Hicks, *Yet Will I Trust Him*, p. 154.
[3]Ibid., p. 304.
[4]Oswald Chambers, *Baffled to Fight Better: Job and the Problem of Suffering* (Grand Rapids, Mich.: Discovery House, 1931), p. 29.
[5]Giacomo Carissimi, *Oratorios and Motets,* Hassler Concert, cond. Franz Raml, trans. and ed. Irmlind Capelle, copyright 1998, MDG 614 0753-2.

Chapter 15: Do You Know When the Mountain Goats Give Birth?

[1]Portions of this story were first published in Howard Spiro, Mary Curnen and Lee Wandel, eds. *Facing Death: Where Culture, Religion and Medicine Meet* (New Haven, Conn.: Yale University Press, 1996) and are reprinted here with permission.

Chapter 16: Can You Pull In the Leviathan with a Fishhook?

[1]Rebecca Manley Pippert, *Out of the Saltshaker* (Downers Grove, Ill.: InterVarsity Press, 1979), p. 158.

[2]Johannes Brahms, *ein deutsches Requiem,* translation mine.

Chapter 17: Things Too Wonderful for Job to Have Known

[1]Chambers, *Baffled to Fight Better,* p. 121.

Epilogue

[1]Joseph Roth, *Job: The Story of a Simple Man* (New York: Viking, 1931).

[2]Ibid., p. 254.

[3]Ibid., p. 266.

[4]Ibid., p. 279.

[5]Eugene O'Neill, *The Great God Brown,* act 4, scene 1 (1926).

Resources

Good books go too rapidly out of print. If that is the case for any resource listed here, try interlibrary loan, used book stores or Internet auctions to find them.

Prologue: Job's Regular Custom
Complementary Concepts:

Valerie Bell, *Getting Out of Your Children's Faces and into Their Hearts* (Grand Rapids, Mich.: Zondervan, 1995). *Job gives us some tips on the spiritual care of our children. Valerie Bell offers some concrete illustrations of how to implement that today.*

Jill Briscoe, *It Had to Be Monday: Personal Reflections on the Life of Job* (Wheaton, Ill.: Tyndale House, 1995). *The author hesitated to write this book because she knew her own children weren't perfect. Fortunately her husband advised her not to wait until their children were spiritual giants because "giants are freaks." She says she learned "to tell Satan to get lost" and got on writing this book.*

Sacred Sounds:

"There was a man in the land of Uz," from *Job*, Sir Charles Hubert Parry, composer, Hilary Davan Wetton conducting the Guildford Choral Society and the Royal Philharmonic Orchestra (Hyperion; CDA67025). *Following a short pastoral motif, the narrator introduces the story of Job in recitative. Composed in the nineteenth century.*

Persuasive Portraits:

Job and His Family, in William Blake, *Illustrations for the Book of Job* (New York: Dover, 1995), p. 2. *In the first engraving of his series on Job, Blake paints a perfect, pious family portrait, but he pencils these New Testament words in beneath Job, his wife and his children: "The Letter Killeth. The Spirit Giveth Life. It is Spiritually Discerned."*

Chapter 1: Enter the Accuser
Complementary Concepts:

David Watson, *Fear No Evil* (Wheaton, Ill.: Harold Shaw, 1992). *The memoir of a pastor with cancer. Watson believes that Job's comforters carried out Satan's work of condemnation.*

M. Scott Peck, *People of the Lie: Hope for Healing Human Evil* (New York: Simon & Schuster, 1983). *Most of us will see the work of Satan carried out by evil people. Peck's investigation into the My Lai massacre of civilians by American military in the Viet Nam War helped him develop a psychology of human evil and a hope for its healing.*

Sacred Sounds:
"Prologo in Cielo," from *Mefistophele,* Arrigo Boito, composer, Nicolai Ghiaurov as Mefistophele, Oliviero de Fabritiis conducting the National Philharmonic Orchestra, (London; 410 175-12). *If you want to know what an angel choir would sound like, this is the piece to listen to. Composed in the nineteenth century.*

Persuasive Portraits:
The Sons of God Came to Present Themselves Before the Lord, and Satan Came Also Among Them, in Arthur Szyk, *The Book of Job with Pictures by Arthur Szyk* (New York: Heritage Press, 1946), p. 78. *Szyk's illuminations for a King James Version of the* Book of Job *use bright colors to create an authentic Middle Eastern flavor. The "sons of God" in this painting appear not as angels but as ordinary people from ordinary professions in life.*

Chapter 2: Disaster Heaped on Disaster
Complementary Concepts:
Stephen Mitchell, *The Book of Job* (New York: Harper, 1979). *The most controversial recent translation of the* Book of Job *is also one of the most provocative commentaries in print. With Job, Mitchell yearns for the Living Redeemer.*

Janice Harris Lord, *No Time for Goodbyes: Coping with Sorrow, Anger and Injustice After a Tragic Death* (Channel Islands, Calif.: Pathfinder, 1987). *This book is especially useful for families like Job's who have lost young adult children suddenly and violently. Unlike most of the families in my practice, they have had no time for the blessings of "anticipatory grief."*

Sacred Sounds:
"Naked I came from my mother's womb," from *Job: An Oratorio,* Sir Peter Maxwell Davies, composer and conductor of the Vancouver Bach Choir and CBC Vancouver Orchestra, Paul Moore, tenor (Collins; 15162). *This modern oratorio uses the texts of Stephen Mitchell's translation of the* Book of Job. *Composed in the twentieth century.*

Persuasive Portraits:
The fire of God is fallen from heaven, and hath burned up the sheep, in Arthur Szyk, *The Book of Job with Pictures by Arthur Szyk* (New York: Heritage Press, 1946), p. 47. *Szyk vividly pictures lightning chasing the sole servant remaining alive down a valley of dead sheep.*

Chapter 3: The Case of the Wannabe Widow
Complementary Concepts:
Muriel Spark, *The Only Problem* (Franklin Center, Penn.: Franklin Library, 1984).

The author of The Prime of Miss Jean Brodie *presents Job's story in a modern parable. Rather than offering a line-by-line analogy, Sharp moves in and out of problems in our daily newspapers.*

Madeleine L'Engle, *Two-Part Invention: The Story of a Marriage* (San Francisco: HarperCollins, 1988). *In sharp contrast to the portraits of Mrs. Job presented in the various fictional works cited, one of our greatest living Christian writers shares her thoughts about the suffering of her own husband from cancer.*

Sacred Sounds:

"Variations on a Theme from Vaughan William's *Job*," from *The Power of the Cello,* Elizabeth Maconchy, composer, Anthony Cooke, cellist. (Harmonie; LC 1761). *So small is Mrs. Job's contribution to the text and so unflattering are the few verses where she expresses her opinion that no musical composer has offered her a song or a movement of their work! To fill that gap I offer a composition based on Job written by a female composer. Composed in the twentieth century.*

Persuasive Portraits:

Job et sa femme, George de la Tour, c. 1635. Part of the permanent collection of the museum in Epinal, France. *This remarkable painting can be seen on the internet at* <*http://sgwww.epfl.ch/BERGER/LaTour/job.htm*>.

Chapter 4: Empathic Failures
Complementary Concepts:

Judith Allen Shelly, *Spiritual Care: A Guide for Caregivers* (Downers Grove, Ill.: InterVarsity Press, 2000). *As a team, Job's comforters got it wrong. If you and your team would like to get it right, Shelly's book on group building is a good place to start.*

Shiela Cassidy, *Sharing the Darkness: The Spirituality of Caring* (London: Dartman, Longman & Todd, 1988). *The medical director of an English hospice talks about the cost of discipleship in caring for those who suffer.*

Sacred Sounds:

"Dance of the Job's Comforters," in *Job: A Masque for Dancing,* Ralph Vaughan Williams, composer, Vernon Handley conducting the London Philharmonic Orchestra (EMI; CD-CFP 4603). *This ballet suite was composed as a musical treatment of William Blake's illustrations to the* Book of Job. *A "masque" traditionally includes all the arts— dance, mime, speech, singing and music. The generous use of pizzicato strings suggests that Job's friends didn't sit very still. Composed in the twentieth century.*

Persuasive Portraits:

Job and His Friends, by Taddeo Gaddi, 1367, Camposanto, Pisa in Samuel Terrien, *The Iconography of JOB Through the Centuries,* (University Park, Penn.: Penn State Press, 1996), p. 96. *Italian fresco that compares Job's skin disease and suffering to the boils and toils of fourteenth-century bubonic plague victims.*

Chapter 5: Job Wishes He Had Never Been Born
Complementary Concepts:

Merton P. Strommen and A. Irene Strommen, *Five Cries of Grief: One Family's Journey to Healing After the Tragic Death of a Son* (Minneapolis: Augsburg, 1996). *We hear alternating voices of mom and dad in this helpful book about healing after the sudden, accidental death of the authors' adult son.*

Philip Yancey, *Where Is God When It Hurts?* (Grand Rapids, Mich.: Zondervan, 1977). *The second section of this classic is titled "How People Respond to Extreme Pain." It presents a range of human responses to Job-like circumstances.*

Sacred Sounds:

"Job's Curse," in *Purcell Realizations: Harmonia Sacra*, Benjamin Britten, composer, Simon Keenlyside, baritone, Graham Johnson, pianist (Hyperion; CDA67061/2). *If I wanted to choose one musical piece to be performed at a program on Job, this would be a good choice. Job's lament that he was ever born borrows from Purcell's original tune and Jeremy Taylor's exquisitely rhymed translation of Job's text. Composed in the twentieth century.*

Persuasive Portraits:

They Saw That His Grief Was Very Great. After This Job Opened His Mouth, and Cursed His Day, in Arthur Szyk, *The Book of Job with Pictures by Arthur Szyk* (New York: Heritage Press, 1946), p. 29. *A naked old man covered with red blotches, Job kneels in a bed of bones as his friends shrink back from the sight of him.*

Chapter 6: On Suicide Watch
Complementary Concepts:

Max Cleland, *Strong at the Broken Places* (New York: Berkeley Books, 1982). *In Viet Nam a hand grenade blew off both of Max Cleland's legs and one of his arms. There were those present who thought the young soldier was better off dead. Instead, Senator Cleland fought despair and emerged as a national political voice for the handicapped. An excellent argument against assisted suicide as a reasonable option.*

Stanley Hauerwas, *Naming the Silences: God, Medicine and the Problem of Suffering* (Grand Rapids, Mich.: Eerdmans, 1990). *Job would have done well if Hauerwas had been one of his visiting friends. This theologian, who is at home in the world of modern medicine, understands better than Eliphaz, Bildad, Zophar and Elihu how to comfort a man like Job.*

Sacred Sounds:

"Muß nicht der Mensch immer im Streit sein" (Does not man have hard service) in *Georg Schumann Choral Music*, Mark Ford conducting the Purcell Singers (ASV; CD DCA 1091). *One of three motets for mixed choir and organ that Schumann wrote on texts from Job, this lovely piece is based on Job 7. Composed in the twentieth century.*

Persuasive Portraits:

Job: My Lament Is a Success, Francis Gruber, oil on canvas, 1944, Tate Gallery, London, in Samuel Terrien, *The Iconography of Job Through the Centuries* (University Park, Penn.: Penn State Press, 1996), p. 250. *Seated naked on a stool in a bombed-out garret reminiscent of World War II Montmartre, Job stares at the floor. Just outside his line of vision is a scroll with Job 23:2 inscribed on it in French which can be translated, "Even now my lament is a success, and yet . . . "*

Chapter 7: The Problem of Argument
Complementary Concepts:

David W. Augsburger, *Caring Enough to Confront* (Ventura, Calif.: Gospel Light, 1981). *Although none of Job's characters lacked the ability to confront those with whom they disagreed, each of them sometimes lacked the ability to care deeply about their partner in conversation. In this book Augsburger introduces his highly useful concept of "carefrontation" that helps us keep both issue and relationships in balance as we work things through.*

Elisabeth Kübler-Ross, *On Death and Dying* (New York: Macmillan, 1969). *Although the author uses stepwise stages of death that do not match practical experience in a linear fashion, this book is a landmark work that illustrates that when it comes to facing loss, we are not all at the same place at the same time.*

Sacred Sounds:

"Lectio secunda (Job 10:1-7)" and "Lectio tertia (Job 10:8-12)" in *Sacrae Lectiones ex Propheta Job,* Roland de Lassus, composer, performed by Cori Spezzati. *Plain chant style lends an appropriately somber mood to Job's complaint about his life. Composed in the sixteenth century.*

Persuasive Portraits:

Seated Job in Profile, oil on canvas by Diego Velázquez, c. 1618-1630, Art Institute of Chicago, in Samuel Terrien, *The Iconography of Job Through the Centuries,* (University Park, Penn.: Penn State Press, 1996), p 150. *Seated alone in the darkness, backlight illuminating his face, back, arm and legs, Job prays in protest.*

Chapter 8: Worthless Physicians
Complementary Concepts:

Paul W. Pruyser, *The Minister as Diagnostician: Personal Problems in Pastoral Perspective* (Philadelphia: Westminster Press, 1976). *Rather than borrowing the language of psychobabble, Pruyser presents clinically useful themes of spiritual diagnosis: (1) awareness of the Holy; (2) providence, (3) faith, (4) gratefulness, (5) repentance. Highly recommended to medical practitioners as well as spiritual counselors.*

Henri Nouwen, *The Wounded Healer: Ministry in Contemporary Society* (Garden City, N.J.: Image Books, 1972). *One of Nouwen's most beloved books helps "worthwhile physicians" see themselves as wounded as their Jobs are.*

Sacred Sounds:

"Agnus Dei," in *Requiem Mass,* John Rutter, composer and conductor of the Cambridge Singers and City of London Sinfonia, (Collegium; COL 103). *Rutter adds Job's words, "Man that is born of a woman hath but a short time to live" (14:1-2) to the traditional requiem mass. Composed in the twentieth century.*

Persuasive Portraits:
The Just Upright Man Is Laughed to Scorn, William Blake, engraving, 1825, in *Blake's Illuminations of the Book of Job,* Illustration No. 10. *Job's worthless physicians use both hands to point in accusation at the suffering man.*

Chapter 9: Empty Notions
Complementary Concepts:
Harold S. Kushner, *When Bad Things Happen to Good People* (New York: Schocken, 1981). *Whether or not you agree with Kushner's view of a distant but growing God, this book is a must-read for those counseling innocent sufferers. If you've never read this book, chances are your Jobs have at least heard of it.*

Granger Westberg, *Good Grief: A Constructive Approach to the Problem of Loss* (Philadelphia: Fortress, 1962). *The beauty of this little book is that it is little—sixty-four slim pages. A valuable resource to offer someone who doesn't have the concentration power to make it through longer offerings.*

Sacred Sounds:
"Interstellar Horncall," in *Cornissimo,* Olivier Messiaen, composer, Gregory Cass, horn player, (Gallo; CD 741). *An explicitly Christian composer, Messiaen draws on Job 16:18 ("O earth, do not cover my blood; may my cry never be laid to rest!") to set a horn solo inspired by Utah's Bryce Canyon. Composed in the twentieth century.*

Persuasive Portraits:
Job's Friends in Dunce Cap, wood sculpture by Robert Falaise, 1522, Miséricorde, Champeaux, Seine-et-Marne, Caisse Nationale des Monuments Historique et des Sites, in Samuel Terrien, *The Iconography of JOB Through the Centuries* (University Park, Penn.: Penn State Press, 1996), p. 125. *Their three heads coifed with one comprehensive dunce cap, Eliphaz, Bildad and Zophar were sculpted with donkey or pig ears to remind sixteenth-century French people of the conceits of Sorbonne theologians.*

Chapter 10: Unfavored Merit
Complementary Concepts:
Philip Yancey, *What's So Amazing About Grace?* (Grand Rapids, Mich.: Zondervan, 1998). *Of particular interest in the context of Job is the fourteenth chapter that deals with "Loopholes."*

Mike Mason, *The Gospel According to Job* (Wheaton, Ill.: Crossway, 1994). *Mason's book dips deeply into the New Testament in commenting on an Old Testament saint. On the other hand, Stephen Mitchell couldn't resist the "radiant large hearted verse" of Jesus of Nazareth either.*

Sacred Sounds:

"I Know That My Redeemer Liveth," in *Messiah*, Georg Friederich Handel, composer. *Most of the world is familiar with this Job's yearning for vindication through Handel's beloved soprano aria that identifies it as a messianic text. Composed in the eighteenth century.*

Persuasive Portraits:

Job With Background of Geometricized Christ à la Cimbauë in Samuel Terrien, *The Iconography of Job Through the Centuries* (University Park, Penn.: Penn State Press, 1996). *Russian-Jewish painter Marc Chagall drew on many biblical themes but never painted Job until the Holocaust brought him face to face with the enormity of evil in the world.*

Chapter 11: Night Vision
Complementary Concepts:

Gerhard E. Frost, *The Color of the Night: Reflections on Suffering and the Book of Job* (Minneapolis: Augsburg, 1977). *Excellent and well-written short meditations on what the author calls the "Matterhorn of the Old Testament."*

Diane M. Komp, *Bedtime Snacks for the Soul: Meditations to Sweeten Your Dreams* (Grand Rapids, Mich.: Zondervan, 2000). *Nighttime devotionals, often drawn from the stories of modern Jobs, written especially for those who find themselves running on empty at bedtime.*

Sacred Sounds:

"Job: Une Sacra Rappresentazione," in *Il Prigioniero*, Luigi Dallapiccola, composer, Ettore Cracis conducting the orchestra and chorus of Teatro la Fenice (Mondo Musica; MFOH 10603). *There are nightmarish qualities to this speech-punctuated sacred musical drama of Job by a posttonal composer. Composed in the twentieth century.*

Persuasive Portraits:

Job's Evil Dreams, watercolor by William Blake, Butts Set No. 11, 1825, in *Blake's Illustrations for the Book of Job* (Mineola, N.Y.: Dover, 1995), p 36. *In a nightmarish watercolor, God visits Job. In this nightmare, God and Satan are indistinguishable.*

Chapter 12: Can a Mortal Be of Use to God?
Complementary Concepts:

Carol Luebering, *Job & Julian of Norwich: Trusting That All Will Be Well* (Cincinnati: St. Anthony Press, 1995). *Luebering offers a seven-day retreat in which she imagines Job meeting a fourteenth-century mystic. At the age of thirty-one, Julian of Norwich took vows as a layperson that included celibacy and obedience but not solitude. To the window of her cell that faced the churchyard, townspeople came to share their stories. There she prayed with more than one Job.*

Sheldon Vanauken, *A Severe Mercy: Davy's Edition* (San Francisco: Harper & Row, 1977). *C. S. Lewis's wife, Joy Davidson, had a profound effect on his Christian writings. One of Lewis's friends, Vanauken, tells the story of his love for his own wife and her death from cancer.*

Sacred Sounds:
"How can a man be pure or a son of woman sinless," in *Job: An Oratorio*, Sir Peter Maxwell Davies, composer and conductor of the Vancouver Bach Choir and CBC Vancouver Orchestra, Paul Moore, tenor. (Collins; 15162). *Twice before Eliphaz said it, and now Bildad repeats this phrase about universal sinfulness. After hearing this accusation, Job repeats his desire to present his case to God. Composed in the twentieth century.*

Persuasive Portraits:
Job and His Comforters, an oil on canvas by Luca Giordano, c. 1960, Tate Gallery, London, in Samuel Terrien, *The Iconography of Job Through the Centuries* (University Park, Penn.: Penn State Press, 1996), p. 186. *Job's weight rests on his left hand as he moves back from his three accusers. On the other hand, "Luke the Quick" painted the three friends arguing among themselves and disinterested in Job.*

Chapter 13: Job's Tears
Complementary Concepts:
Nicholas Wolterstorff, *Lament for a Son* (Grand Rapids, Mich.: Eerdmans, 1987). *A powerful personal memoir of grief that offers the honest tears of a dad rather than the easy answers of a classroom-bound philosopher.*

Luci Shaw, *God in the Dark: Through Grief and Beyond* (Vancouver: Regent College, 1998). *A Christian poet shares eloquently about her husband's death from cancer.*

Sacred Sounds:
"Requiem: Eric Wolterstorff in Memorium," Cary Ratcliff, composer. *Commissioned by the Wolterstorff family in honor of their son, the texts of the six sections are included as an appendix to* Lament for a Son. *First performed May 19, 1986, in Grand Rapids, Michigan. Composed in the twentieth century.*

Persuasive Portraits:
Job and the Angel of Death, Marc Chagall, tinted drawing, 1960, in Samuel Terrien, *The Iconography of Job Through the Centuries* (University Park: Pennsylvania State University Press, 1996), p. 259. *Overcome by the presence of evil, Job lies prostrate on the ground as his three comforters retreat into the background.*

Chapter 14: A Generational Clash
Complementary Concepts:
Edwin H. Friedman, *Generation to Generation: Family Process in Church and Synagogue* (New York: Guilford, 1986). *When a Job is a member of a family of faith, the real-life story of innocent suffering impacts an entire congregation. Rabbi Friedman uses concepts of family systems therapy to discuss problem-solving in congregational life.*

Ron Zemke, Claire Raines and Bob Filpczak, *Generations at Work: Managing the*

Clash of Veterans, Boomers, Xers, and Nexters in Your Workplace (New York: AMACOM, 2000). *The shared values of a generation may have as much impact on how a team member problem solves as age, worldview or experience.*

Sacred Sounds:

"Elihu's Dance of Youth and Beauty," from *Job: A Masque for Dancing*, Ralph Vaughan Williams, composer, Vernon Handley conducting the London Philharmonic Orchestra (EMI; CD-CFP 4603). *The seventh movement of Vaughan Williams's ballet suite features a haunting solo violin. Composed in the twentieth century.*

Persuasive Portraits:

Job and Elihu, ninth-century illumination, Saint John Monastery, Patmos, in Samuel Terrien, *The Iconography of Job Through the Centuries: Artists as Biblical Interpreters* (University Park: Pennsylvania State University Press, 1996), p. 36. *In this illumination for a Greek codex of the* Book of Job, *the artist presents Elihu as a dramatic transition from the three older friends' debates.*

Chapter 15: Do You Know When the Mountain Goats Give Birth?
Complementary Concepts:

George A. Maloney, *Alone with the Alone: An Eight-Day Retreat* (Notre Dame, Ind.: Ave Maria Press, 1982). *An excellent way to contemplate God's questions that he posed to Job.*

John Mark Hicks, *Yet Will I Trust Him: Understanding God in a Suffering World* (Joplin, Mo.: College Press, 1999). *Hicks wrote about Job's story after his own wife's death and while his son was terminally ill. Even with these losses he recognizes what every mountain goat knows: "God's creation is not the playground of his power but the nursery of his care."*

Sacred Sounds:

"Job: Mystery of Creation" from *The Organ Music of Petr Eben*, Petr Eben, composer, Halgier Schiager, organist (Hyperion; CDA67194). *Like Boito, Czech composer Eben noted the similarities between Faust and Job, the suffering of his native people and the suffering of Job. "The Mystery of Creation" opens* pianissimo *with the still, small voice of God. Composed in the twentieth century.*

Persuasive Portraits:

When the Morning Stars Sang Together by William Blake, Butts Set. #14 in *Blake's Illustrations for the Book of Job* (Mineola, N.Y.: Dover, 1995), p. 37. *In a stunning watercolor, Job and his family crouch in a cave above which God and his angels shine forth. Although the cave ceiling is solid and opaque, Job and his wife and children sense what is going on above their heads.*

Chapter 16: Can You Pull In the Leviathan with a Fishhook?
Complementary Concepts:

Eugene Peterson, *Job: The Message* (Colorado Springs: NavPress, 1996). *Always playful, sometimes cheeky, Peterson's contemporary rendering of* Job *is worth a read-through all on its own.*

Oswald Chambers, *Baffled to Fight Better: Job and the Problem of Suffering* (Grand Rapids, Mich.: Discovery House, 1931). *Interesting reflections on the Book of* Job *by the author of* My Utmost for His Highest.

Sacred Sounds:
"Scene IV," from *Job,* Sir Charles Hubert Parry, composer, Hilary Davan Wetton conducting the Guildford Choral Society and the Royal Philharmonic Orchestra (Hyperion: CDA67025). *The most delightful and exciting choral portion of Parry's oratorio is a rehearsal of creation. Composed in the nineteenth century.*

Persuasive Portraits:
Antichrist Riding Leviathan, a twelfth-century illumination in Oxford University's Bodelian Library collection, in Samuel Terrien, *The Iconography of Job Through the Centuries: Artists as Biblical Interpreters* (University Park: Pennsylvania State University Press, 1996), p. 47. *Fearsome creatures such as leviathan, behemoth and rahab are linked with evil throughout Scripture.*

Chapter 17: Things Too Wonderful for Job to Have Known
Complementary Concepts:
J. B. Phillips, *Your God Is Too Small* (New York: Macmillan, 1960). *An English classic that contrasts the destructive unreal gods we substitute for the mountain goats' Midwife and the leviathan's Fisherman.*

Ric Ergenbright, *The Art of God: The Heavens & the Earth* (Wheaton, Ill.: Tyndale House, 1999). *If your Job is house- or hospital-bound and cannot enjoy nature directly, this coffee-table book by a renowned landscape photographer blends some of those things too wonderful for Job to have known along with scientific observations and parallel Scripture quotations.*

Sacred Sounds:
"O, daß ich wäre, wie in den Tagen" ("Oh That I Were As in the Days") from *Georg Schumann Choral Music,* Mark Ford conducting the Purcell Singers (ASV; CD DCA 1091). *In the final of Schumann's three motets for mixed choir and organ, Job, once the most popular religious teacher in the city square, mourns his loss of respect. Composed in the twentieth century.*

Persuasive Portraits:
Steve Terrill, *Wonder of It All: The Creation Account According to the Book of Job* (Los Angeles: New Leaf Press, 2000). *Terrill uses nature photography to illustrate the conversation between God and Job about creation.*

Epilogue: A Song of Restoration
Complementary Concepts:

Arthur W. Frank, *The Wounded Storyteller: Body, Illness and Ethics* (Chicago: University of Chicago Press, 1996). *A professor of sociology who survived both cancer and heart disease explores the value of storytelling in a "remission society" made up of those living with uncertainty. Of particular interest to Job's restoration is Frank's concept of "the restitution narrative."*

Peter Kreeft, *Making Sense Out of Suffering* (Ann Arbor, Mich.: Servant, 1986). *Clues to the problem of suffering from philosophers, artists and prophets.*

Sacred Sounds:

"Historia di Job" from *Oratorios and Motets,* Giacomo Carissimi, composer, Franz Raml conducting the Hassler Consort (Scene DG; MDG614 0753-2). *More a sacred conversation than a full oratorio. The story of Job is presented through three voices: Job, Satan and God's angel. In the final movement, a cursing Satan is banished by blessing. In triumphantly lyric contrast to Satan, Job and the angel close with the blessing of God's name on their lips. Composed in the seventeenth century.*

Persuasive Portraits:

Job Intercedes for His Friends, Bernard van Orley, oil on canvas, c. 1521-1525, Musées Royaux des Beaux-Arts, Brussels, in Samuel Terrien, *The Iconography of Job Through the Centuries: Artists as Biblical Interpreters* (University Park, Penn.: Penn State Press, 1996), p. 164. *Part of an altarpiece commissioned by Margaret of Austria, Regent of the Low Countries, and gift to the Count of Lalaing. A restored Job stands in splendid dress at a higher level than his humiliated kneeling friends. The artist invites us to emulate Job and pray for others, even when we think they are in a lower state of life or grace than our own.*